G' STER

GANG LIFE TO GREAT LIFE

NANO S.

authorHOUSE®

AuthorHouse™
1663 Liberty Drive
Bloomington, IN 47403
www.authorhouse.com
Phone: 833-262-8899

Published by AuthorHouse 10/12/2022

ISBN: 978-1-6655-7281-1 (sc)
ISBN: 978-1-6655-7282-8 (e)

Library of Congress Control Number: 2022918571

Print information available on the last page.

CONTENTS

Acknowledgements vii
Introduction..ix
This Book is dedicated to My Mother & Father xi
Foreword..xiii

Chapter 1 1
Chapter 2 9
Chapter 3 15
Chapter 4 20
Chapter 5 27
Chapter 6 35
Chapter 7 44
Chapter 8 51
Chapter 9 59
Chapter 10 71
Chapter 11 75
Chapter 12 81
Chapter 13 86
Chapter 14 90

About The Author 99
Epilogue... 101
Contact 103

ACKNOWLEDGEMENTS

To acknowledge every single person for making it possible to even be in the position to write this book would be a book in itself. So to start I'd like to acknowledge "The Boys" and everyone that lived in the neighborhood. Mad P.C. on the corner. Mrs. G down the street. The Big Guy for being so cool. The list goes on and on. I'd like to give credit to some professionals that don't get enough, the SDFD. You guys save countless lives everyday behind the bullshit that goes on in the streets, for that Thank You.

Then there are those that weren't from the neighborhood, people I met during my adventures. I met quite a few people in my life and some of them had a real big influence on it, some bad, some good but all with heart. My children, whom have been so supportive of this project, and to all those who never said no, much love and respect but most importantly thank you, thank you. Without you there'd be no me.

To my brothers and sisters for putting up with most of my bullshit, to those that died on the field of battle, to those that got sent to the Big House and to those still on the street. Love, Miss & Respect you.

A special thanks to my sponsors, you've been with me through this whole process.

INTRODUCTION

America's Finest City… A nickname like that conjures up beautiful beaches, fine dining & entertainment. My home city of San Diego is known for that moniker, yet I grew up in an entirely different city than the one with beautiful beaches; I grew up on the mean streets of Southeast San Diego, home to some of the roughest street gangs in California. Gangs with ties to drug cartels and prison gangs with access to all sorts of shit, but this isn't about them this is about one young kid (like many before him and after him) that went into this world knowing but not knowing and walked with the devil for years.

Aside from a few broken bones and scars, I found a way to bring myself back from this violent, drug induced lifestyle, and lead a productive life. Became the father a man is supposed to be to his children, the brother to his siblings, and a trusted employee. This story is proof that there is hope out there no matter how bad life kicks your ass…..

I'm pretty sure life has done a number on many people far worse than it did to me.

THIS BOOK IS DEDICATED TO MY MOTHER & FATHER

There was no way you could have known what I would become, but you both gave me the tools to live, survive and thrive in this world. I would never have had the courage and wisdom without the guidance you gave me while I was still a good kid; I never forgot the lessons although I did put them on hold for a while. I thank you for being the good people your parents taught you to be. I thank you moms for being the rock of our family for all those years and to my dad I thank you for the vicious left hook you taught me. The respect, honor, and loyalty you showed one another is the cement that holds our family together to this day.

FOREWORD

Ever since I was a wee lad, I remember my father being a gangster, and I don't mean this new age version where an old lady listening to Snoop is considered 'gangster'. I mean the real thing, true to life 'Gang Member' from a notorious group of thugs. He was more than a member though; they followed him into battle like soldiers following a great general (When generals would actually fight alongside their troops). I saw men and women willing to do anything to gain his favor, out of a mixture of fear and respect. They feared him because he was absolute violence embodied in a thin Mexican frame. Aimed and trained violence with no fear, no hesitation, and no remorse. They respected him because he never beat up anyone that didn't have it coming. He ruled our small neighborhood with an iron fist. Akin to a king over a small kingdom, I remember being called "Gangland Royalty". He wasn't a greedy man who coveted power like most in that type of position. He was content with his but would also defend it to no end.

Our neighborhood was ours. It was his. I saw people walking down our street, and if he was standing outside, they would just cross the street and cross the street once they passed him. I knew with a man like that on my side I would be just fine. I'm not saying it was all cookies and milk. We definitely struggled. He spent a lot of time in jail and prisons and his lifestyle wasn't always accepted. Our family life was turbulent to say the least, but we were a strong family with a strong leader. Not him but my grandmother. I see now that he learned to make hard decisions and work with very little watching her as she raised 5 of her 7 children, (2 of my uncles had left home way before I came along), after my grandfather passed away very early. Wherever his inspiration came from, he reached a level not many get to and even less get to live through.

Being the son of a Gangland king was an adventure all its own. An adventure filled with tragedy, sorrow, and violence. I wouldn't change a thing though. The lessons learned can't be found in a classroom anywhere on earth. I learned to be strong, fair, ruthless, but compassionate, and how to earn respect. Rather than think it is a thing given freely. My time as gangland royalty was a unique time that I look back on both cherishingly and feel relieved of. It was nice feeling the warm embrace of the subjects in our small kingdom. The fear of rivals coming in was always there but the armed guards at the gate usually intercepted any unwanted guests. The relief if it isn't obvious is the risk of getting shot or jumped by rivals or anyone for that matter has decreased exponentially!

T Mojito,
Husband, Father, Business Owner & Musician, San Diego, CA
Cheers!

CHAPTER

After my 10th birthday, I knew things would never be the same for me. Innocence lost some would say. But not me, I was well aware of what I was getting into. Being the youngest of 7 kids was kind of cool. My parents (God rest their souls) were decent folk from the old country, moms was from the hills of Monterey, Mexico. My father, rumor had it, was from the same town as the famed Mexican Revolutionary Pancho Villa. 'Land of the Scorpion' is one of the nicknames for the area, but it was all deserts to my young eyes when I saw the place myself except for this statue of Pancho Villa himself, sitting on a horse right there in the middle of the desert. Biggest damn statue I'd ever seen. Aside from the hot bright days, it was an experience I would never forget. I always wondered why my father spoke of it so fondly.

Talk about a place time forgot, I remember seeing bullet holes on the walls of the clay buildings. The first day there my dad took me into the middle of the village, a dusty road with 2 cantinas facing each other; one was named "El Coyote" & the other "El Gallo". His was El Gallo so we sauntered in the bar and upon entering the bartender a burly o'l Mexican looked up from the bar and shouts "Bernardo!" which blew me away because as far as I knew my dad hadn't been there in years. But the guy seemed genuinely happy to see my dad. We walked up to the bar, and they exchange pleasantries, and the guy looks at me and says in

Spanish, "who's this little runt?' My dad says "es mi hijo" the bartender says "sit his ass right here" pointing to a barstool.

So, my dad motions me up on the stool. The guy asks me "gustas una soda?" nodding my head I said "coca por favor". Now for some reason Mexican soda is much stronger than American soda, even though it's the same company. Shit just stronger deep down south.

One thing about my parents though, they had very different opinions of 'ole Mexico. My father loved it whereas my dear mother hated it. But it's safe to say they both loved America's Finest City. Moving right along. In 1974 the neighborhood of my youth was rife with racism and the start of gang violence.

To this day I still don't know how we became a "Street Gang" But somewhere between Bugs Bunny and Happy Days the guys I grew up with were documented by the police and the newly formed gang detail as "Gang Members". This unit of elite police officers was made up of guys who were bullied themselves during their time in elementary school and found a way to get back at the bullies. Some with a serious hard-on for young gang members, for those unfortunate enough to have run-ins with them were met with regular ass kicking's, or a little time in juvie. But the game of cat and mouse went on. Never a dull moment in the neighborhood.

The King of the neighborhood was this big cat called "T" it was short for Rube. A smooth fella of the time, with long, slick black hair combed back, and two fists that were quick to bust a fool in the mouth. He had been steadily beating up people for the hood since he was 13. I never saw anyone that enjoyed socking people up like I did with "T". This guy beat the hell out of 3 guys once for drinking a couple of his beers. The cool thing about that was he didn't break their faces because they were from the neighborhood after all, but he did bruise their ribs to no end.

Another time I saw him calmly walk up to a guy (Big ass mother too) right as the fighting was breaking out at the park. I was walking home one night taking a short cut when I saw my older homeboy arguing with some black dudes. As I approached them, he whispered to me to get out of there as he was ready to stab the guy and he showed me a knife in his pocket.

I ran the 2 short blocks to a spot where some older fellas hung out and told them a homie was in trouble at the park, as they drove there, and I ran back. I saw as he proceeded to smash the guy with a bumper jack across the shoulder. Bumper jacks & crowbars were weapons of choice back then. Well, as anyone could guess that ended that fight.

No one was allowed to steal things out of people's back yards. Or mess with kids and old folks. Things like that. "T" made sure of that and dealt with anyone who disrespected the neighborhood. I know this might sound like an old Italian movie but it's not, it's just the way it is in the hood. "T" took a liking to me as a little kid running around the block on my bike or homemade go cart. I was kind of a smart ass too. But no one could have known then that I would fight him for the kingdom 20 years later. "T" was a wise dude. He was the coolest guy on the block, had the prettiest girlfriend & respect from everyone. If there was a problem "T" was the guy everyone came to. Yes, he was King, and he ruled it rightly so.

We lived in a modest neighborhood open to any passersby and allies alike but a no zone to those who came looking for trouble. House after house of hard-working Mexican families lined the neighborhood. 1974 was a cool time in southern California, especially America's Finest City: Low-rider's were cruising; long hair was worn by both guys and girls. The music was awesome, Stylistics, Blue Magic, The Commodore's to name a few. I myself was into "The Fonz" and "Speed Racer" in his Mach 5.

Either way life for me was OK. Dad worked, mom worked, and I had 4 older siblings at home that kept my parents' attention away from me. My 2 oldest brothers had left home by now. So, I was able to seek and learn on my own. I attended the neighborhood school like everyone else. It was funny because I would get the same teachers my older siblings had, and it was always the same thing: "your brothers didn't behave like this" as if I wanted to be like them.

Not me, no sir! At the age of 10 in the fourth grade my childhood lifestyle took a turn you wouldn't believe. The very essence of my soul was changed. I would go on to see things that no 10-year-old should see, let alone be exposed too. But life is such. I met my best friend that way. As I said earlier, the neighborhood of my youth was rife with racism (we'll get to the gang stuff later). I was in class and this new kid was transferred from another class because he seemed to be a bit of a troublemaker over there.

It was a strange move none-the-less because he was like 13 years old and should have been in a 6th grade class. So, here's this kid... Tall, lanky and with a quiet demeanor about him. I didn't talk to him because, well why would I? But it wasn't more than a day that 2 black guys came in the room and started shit with this tall, lanky kid. He wasn't afraid; he just stood up and picked up a chair and faced his opponents head on.

Me being the knucklehead I was, although I didn't know it at the time, grabbed a chair also and stood next to this tall & lanky kid. Before I continue, I have to admit that back then everybody was tall to me. I stood a little over 4 feet tall. But I came to the aid of this strange young dude who entered my classroom just the day before and here he was facing 2 mayates (that's what we called black kids) with a chair. Kind of cool, I would say.

Without saying a word, he threw the chair at the two black kids and picked up another one, so I just followed suit and threw mine. About 8 to 10 chairs were thrown that day. No one was seriously hurt, but those mayates didn't mess with the tall, lanky kid for at least a week after that. We walked home together that day and every day after that.

A week goes by, and Tony and I were just getting to know each other. We had many things in common, which is odd but what the hell. It was kind of strange that he was 13 and in a 4th grade class but apparently, he had been having trouble all over the school. His last exploit that landed him in my class was he had been seeing a black girl and her cousin was not happy about it at all.

So, this 4th grade teacher took him in and did her best to befriend him. In the long run she did (bless her heart). Although she hated me to no end, (remember I told you I was kind of a smart ass and drove her nuts with my shenanigans). A week later as we were walking out of the school, we were approached by these mayates again. This time Tony didn't hold back, he beat the crap out of one of them and the others just backed down. And so, it went. Tony and I became inseparable; we hung out in the morning, during school, and after school.

Usually at 4 o'clock is when we would split up to go home and watch Speed Racer and eat dinner then we would meet up again until it was time to go home around 9 pm because if he got home any later than that his father would lock the door on him. My parents rarely saw when I would get home, not that they didn't care, but having all those other kids kept them busy. Many a night Tony would sleep in my back yard.

Whatever you might think, this was turning into anything other than a normal friendship. We would be out looking for bikes to steal so we could build our own out of stolen parts. Having a new bike from the store only put a target on you by the other kids. Labeling one a "rich boy" kind of kept you out of the cool guy group. Don't misunderstand, as most of the neighborhood was working class dads and stay at home moms (some moms had to work). You'd be lucky to get a new bike for Christmas. One thing about the old neighborhood: Our Mexican parents sure made a lot of babies. Almost like a race to see who could have more kids. Like I said I came from a family of seven.

Then there was a family around the corner of five brothers and twin sisters. Tragedy would befall some of these families. Another family had so many that I could never remember all their names. But what I do remember is they were all tough as nails, quick to put their fists in any conservation. Hell, one of the sisters even chased one of my brothers' home one day. Of course, he refused to go outside and fight her because he said he wouldn't fight a "girl", but I think he just didn't want to get his ass kicked by a "girl".

Life in the old neighborhood was fun. As in all places though it was divided up by many things and issues mainly by race and back then it was just 2 major parties. Black and Brown! There were a couple of white families also and they were cool as fuck too. Once, we saw a white guy on a motorcycle ride through (not from the neighborhood white families). Unfortunately for him he was struck by a car and as he laid in the street next to the curb, groaning in pain, although we didn't see the actual accident, we came running after hearing it. What we did see was a black dude walk up to him and asked what hurt? He moaned and said he couldn't move. The guy asked, "are you sure?" and when the biker replied "yeah" the brother proceeded to take his wallet!

I did say there was a lot of racism in my neighborhood. But I'm pretty sure it didn't matter what skin color the injured person was, I'm thinking he would have gotten robbed either way.

It wasn't too soon after that these violent actions of ours made us rather popular with the kids in the school & the neighborhood that one day an older fella from the hood was sitting on his porch watching, motioned us over as we walked out of the school, he introduced himself as 'Bugs' (which was short for Bobby, but everyone just called him "Bugs"). Asked if we wanted to see something cool? Of course, we did so we followed him to his garage. Inside among all the spare parts and tools & mostly junk sat the baddest chopper bike we had ever seen.

It had long forks with a small tire in front with whitewalls and a banana seat with a light on the back and a custom Schwinn frame. We admired it, sat on it, and were clearly impressed by it. We had been building dirt bikes with motocross handlebars and thick knobby tires. We would ride our bikes on what we called "Sammy's Trails" named after one of the few white boys in our neighborhood. But this was something new and cool. I might add that he had fashioned a motorcycle battery onto it and an 8-track tape stereo to the bike frame. Something unheard of in those days, but it's true; this guy was way beyond his time. Anyway, he asked us if we would want one. So, after we said "hell yeah" to his question! He said "come back tomorrow and I'll show you how to make one"

Before I continue, I have to tell you about "Bugs". This guy was way older than us. He was at least 18 when we met. But for some reason or another, age in my neighborhood didn't seem to disqualify you from hanging around. If you had what it takes, then you was in, simple as that. Anyway, Bugs didn't pick us out of a hat. Well, if you want to get technical about it, the school could have been a hat!

What I'm saying is that Bugs picked us out of all the kids that passed his house every day. I think he couldn't help it because he lived right across the street from the school entrance. Also, because he had just suffered an auto accident, he was home all day. So, he took an interest in watching all the future of our fine city walking out of the school every day.

You have to understand that back in the 70's there was no internet, so the weirdoes hadn't manifested themselves yet, and it was safe to let kids walk home from school. Some would grow up to be construction workers, others would become lawyers, and a few even became cops. Jaime was one of our good friends. He joined the United States Marine Corps and became a Prison Guard after, but it never stopped us from being friends. Hell, his mom knew my mom.

But the majority of them became drug addicts, burglars, robbers & convicts. Guess which road we took? Something about two odd ball looking kids must have caught his eye. So, from the very beginning of our days with Bugs he was always teaching us something. Of course, I drove him nuts too with my smart-ass remarks and shenanigans but in a way, I think he liked it too, I think for him it showed character from me.

Bugs showed us how to tell time by looking at the sun. A very cool thing I do to this very day. He gave us the gift of time, a useful tool that has saved my ass more than once in this life-time. He literally trained us to be criminals. He would take us on missions, and I have to be honest here, this was the best time of my life! Here I am a 10-year-old kid, didn't even have pubic hair yet, and was sitting on my homemade dirt bike made out of stolen parts on a corner receiving instructions on how much time we had to remove square head lights with frames off a car. I'd like to point out that there were no electric screwdrivers back then; all we had was a good old fashioned Phillips screwdriver.

This type of headlight had just hit the scene and man they sold like hot cakes to all the low-rider guys around the neighborhood and other people Bugs was in contact with. So here we are with tools in hand and a paper grocery bag (man, we were ghetto). Bugs gave us 7 minutes from "go" to be clear of said car. We didn't do it on the first car but trust me we hit several cars in them days and not just for the lights.

We went after stereos, toolboxes, hub caps, batteries, pretty much anything that we could sell to low-rider guys. But in time we could have a set of square lights in the bag and rolling down the street in 7 minutes. To be 10 years old and having a pocket full of money gave me a sense of, well it sure beat the hell out of not having any and Bugs made sure we got our share. Never any shyster shit with him. The man oozed "Honor among Thieves".

That type of thinking didn't come into our heads back then. The corruption didn't start until many, many years down the road. By then it was too late to turn back. Most of our souls were drawn to the dark side. Many friends had been buried, lost to "La Vida Loka" or gone to the big house with an accumulation of thousands of years or Life sentences amongst the lot of them! I'm telling you, that was one vicious ass game we played.

CHAPTER

Thus began the story of "us" and in the following years we would lose freedom, friends & minds but through it all the "Carnalismo" (Brotherhood) we learned those first couple of summers was a bond that would endure all tests of time. There were other fellas who were a part of our little group of, well we didn't exactly know what we could be considered other than we were friends from the neighborhood. To be honest I use the phrase "neighborhood" now so nonchalantly but back then I didn't really know about neighborhoods or the significance of such a word. After all I was only 10! To us were just a bunch of kids, doing kid shit.

We played, experimented with drugs, sniffed paint & drank beer all in due time. We first started off as kids not knowing anything and learned as we went. Like I said Tony was a strange kind of fellow, for starters "Tony Rich" as he would later come to be known by everyone in the hood wasn't a rich boy by far. On the contrary, he was very modest in his living arraignments at home. So, his tastes for luxury grew as time went by, hence the nickname "Tony Rich". Tony had a little brother known to all as "Blue" because of his very light complexion, which gave off a blue tinted shade. He was rather tall for his age, clumsy at times, but sharp as a tack that one was.

Blue loved Tony with all his heart, Tony was his everything, and Tony loved him back. They had a couple sisters, one older and one younger. His dad was a Pachuco (Zoot-Suiter) from East L.A. even wore a "Ducktail Doo" till his dying day. First time I ever met Tonys' dad, he growled at me! I'm serious, I walked up to Tonys' house and "pops" as I would call him from then on was kind of leaning into his truck doing some shit to it and as respectfully as I could I asked if Tony was home?

The man growled at me, and I was like "What the ..." and I just rolled past him. Walked into the back yard which was actually the front of the house; it sat behind a front house where an infamous family lived, although you'll figure that out in a while.

To me Tony was a friend and over the next couple of years we became "brothers" the kind that trusted each other without doubt, that would do anything the other asked without hesitation. That would not run out under any circumstances. Well pretty much. We all became "brothers" to one extent or the other; we never saw what was coming; nor do we blame anyone for what happened. It was the will of the Gods that all that happen, I guess.

Before the summer's end that year I had lost my virginity, stolen cars, and broke into houses. Tony, Bugs & I did many things in those days, we lived on the edge; we took many, many risks. We put ourselves out there, tested our bodies, and put them to their limits. Tony also loved boxing; he was a natural, and I, on the other hand, was too damn short so I was into karate.

As the story goes, Bugs taught us the moves of the criminal underworld, and Tony and I studied how to fight in different styles. Funny thing too that in the short years we spent together we got into one fist fight with each other if you could call it that. That dude had fucking bricks for fists and trust me when I say they hurt like hell when you were on the receiving end of one.

Tony had always been in love with this one chick down the street. Nice girl, with a couple brothers and an older sister. Their mom was hella cool, she liked to drink and listen to Barry Manilow. We would hang out there from time to time and drink some funky Mad Dog 20/20 wine. Tony would disappear to the back with Linda. Like a loyal puppy I would wait until he came out with that shit eating grinning smile of his and say, "Let's go" and off we'd go on another adventure.

By now we usually had shit lined up, bikes had been spotted and marked for taking. Sometimes we met up with Bugs to do some car work, remember Bugs was way older than us so he already had a car (one of the coolest low riders in the neighborhood). Not entirely thanks to us but he got this settlement from his car accident and bought this 1969 Super Sport Impala with skirts and blue metal flake paint job. Add to that the square lights and TV we gave him.

Yes, sir we cruised in style when we weren't out hustling. We'd go to the neighborhood Jack's and buy so much food, then go park on some lonely street and get our grub on while watching TV. We didn't fly under the radar for too long before "T" noticed we were putting in work around the neighborhood. So, he called for us one day, or night I should say. We were reprimanded for bringing "heat" to the neighborhood when those in charge were doing other things. It was all good until "T" decided to hit Tony across the face with a quick jab to get his point across! We were young kids and "T" was a grown ass man and it really bothered me that he felt the need to hit Tony but what could I do?

Don't get me wrong, I understand it now, but I didn't then. Tony took it like a champ and as we were leaving "T" did pull Tony to the side and let him know it was a necessary evil in this world we were now a part of. So, there we were receiving our first lesson in "Neighborhood Etiquette" feeling like we were bullied but such was not the case. I understand that what we did was what one does in our situation but where we did it was not cool in the eyes of those we looked up to.

Soon the summer ended, and we moved up a grade in school (still elementary) now I was taking an interest in girls. Of course, there was a girl. I liked but to her I didn't even exist. Then there was Lena who took my virginity in her front yard. Sure, Tony had Linda and Bugs had a couple here and there. But it seemed like I was destined to be single for the duration of this time period. It was OK though because I was really into other crap.

I was into fighting and always plotting something not to mention that I was the youngest of the trio with Bugs in his early adult years and

Tony about 3 years ahead of me. But age 11 and 12 was fast approaching and our exploits grew and widened as we developed our skills. Not only were we becoming good criminals, we were introduced to the gang way of doing things. Not by choice I might add but by force. Most of the guys in my neighborhood hung out with people their own age 15-year-olds with 15-Year-olds and 16-year-olds with 16-year-olds and so forth.

This is why Tony, Bugs & I were unique, we didn't see the numbers we saw the talent. But either way I knew other kids my age as Tony knew kids his age and Bugs knew the guys his age. One night Tony and I were walking around the neighborhood, huffing paint, a drug I never really liked but did it because Tony did it. We happen to pass by Linda's house and noticed some unknown fellas out front. We walked up to the door and were stopped by 2 "cholos" a term for Mexican gang members. They not only denied us entry into the house but demanded to know where we were from! One of them proceeded to lift Tonys' shirt and asked if he was armed? To this point in my life, I had not seen any reason to carry weapons of any sort. Tony never carried a weapon either. Pretty much any problems we had were solved with fists and feet. Of course, later in life things would be much different. At this point I feel I should I let you know that Tony was one of the most jealous persons in the world! He was very protective of anything he loved including me but, like I said to this point in our life's weapons were never a need for concern.

But this night changed all that for us as we were being accosted by these cholos. We call them that because they dressed funny and talked funny using weird words like "ese" "watcha" and all sorts of other shit. I was actually surprised at these dudes' behavior up to this point, but I guess it was for the best that we learned how to deal with this new madness in our life. One dude lifted Tonys' shirt and said, "you packing ese?" as Tony slapped his hand away and almost whispering "get your fucking hands off me" because once Tony was mad his voice would drop a couple of octaves.

So, as I looked for an escape route. I saw a car with some older neighborhood guys passing by. I flagged them down and told them about these guys messing with us in a way that we didn't quite understand yet. Next thing you know there was this huge crowd in the street facing off with each other! Like I said this gang stuff was new to me and I really didn't understand any of it but, believe you me, I learned that shit real quick. Somebody had handed a crowbar to Tony and as we stood on the sidewalk watching the events unfold some of their guys approached Tony.

One dude caught Tony off guard and punched Tony in the face and as Tony fell back onto me, I pushed him forward and he swung the crowbar hitting the first guy across the jaw (breaking it I'm sure) knocking him into two other guys and knocking all of them down to the ground, a really awesome thing to watch. But then the rest of them decided to pull knives and rush us as the other guys in the street started fighting and yelling out some gang name and how they are number 1. In the end Tony got stabbed with an ice pick and my little ass got chased down the street as they took turns shooting at me while I jumped over cars and ran around the corner.

Once I got away, I didn't find Tony until the next day. Turned out he had run down the alley and went in through Linda's window and she comforted him all night as he soaked a bed sheet with blood. The first of many battle scars he would endure throughout his life. I have to be honest here, this being shot at was a scary thing. Damn bullets make a distinct sound when they whiz over one's head, but it was also a learning thing because it was the first time but certainly would not be the last time, I would have bullets flying around me.

We later found out that Linda's older sister had invited a couple of her friends over for a little kick back and drinking. One girl invited her boyfriend; he then brought along his "homeboys", and they brought along their trouble making friends and the rest went down in gang history. In total no one was shot or killed, but many cars were hit, and windows broken, oh and one of their guys got hit by an oncoming car. From the later stories that came about from that night, for what it's worth, the girl that invited her boyfriend ended up getting socked by somebody on their side. I guess they didn't like the fact that some of their guys got messed up because of her.

I have to admit though that the adrenalin rushing through me that night gave me a new type of rush. I mean up until now I had been training to be a criminal. But to be a gang member is an entirely different kind of animal. You see all gang members are criminals but not all criminals are gang members. And so it went that we were introduced to our first gang fight. Of course, there were many to follow with a whole slew of other gangs in the city, but this one particular night covered just about all that can happen when one gets into this type of shit. Aside from learning that anything can happen at any time I realized that one's' life can come to an abrupt end. This thought really engraved itself into me.

It seems I was bitten by the gang bug hard after that. I decided no one would ever chase me again, although that proved to be wrong by a long shot. I would be chased by other gang members, drug dealer bodyguards, cops and even a concerned citizen from time to time. No one would disrespect my neighborhood ever again! At least not without repercussions, no one would ever cross that line with me or any of my friends or "homeboys". We still didn't know we had become gang members yet.

But something changed after that night, something in our way of thinking about self-preservation, changed maybe for the better or worse because dying for the hood didn't seem to bother anyone, except the parents but we didn't give them much thought until years later. I've learned in my older years that this world is very, very small compared to the normal world we all actually live in. But from this side it's a freaking jungle where just being strong doesn't mean you'll survive! No sir, here in this jungle you got to be quick with your skills as well as your strength.

For example, I was very small for my age and running around these streets like I owned them was a sight to see. Never a day went by that I had to more or less prove I had what it takes to survive! But either way life in the barrio was different. Tony started carrying this old army knife he used as a screwdriver, only now it was for self-defense. I came up on a buck knife and started carrying that. Tony became stricter with his brother Blue too. He wouldn't let him out in the streets after dark.

CHAPTER

We became more in tune with who was walking around the neighborhood or who was at the park and what they were doing there. Remember I said that I learned this shit real quick, because to live the gang life, to see death befall a young man, to attend a funeral that is being watched by "Gang Detail" taking pictures and harassing one as they left the cemetery, can take its toll on one as young as we were. Throughout the years as the gang wars got deep a few stepped back and re-entered civilian life, went back to school, got jobs, got married and went on to live happy and productive lives. Not that we didn't, I'm just saying they did it the normal way. But the gang life did not consume us as you might think, nor did it break some of the bonds that we had built over the first couple of summers we spent together as "kids doing kid shit". Yes, Tony and I were into other stuff, and we conducted ourselves in accordance with our teachings by going on thieving missions with Bugs.

Tony had his boxing & Linda, and I had my Karate. Our lives were pretty full, but now we had areas that were either theirs or ours to deal with. That was a lot of shit going on for young bucks such as us. I even started dressing differently. But our main goal was to make money. And so it went that Tony, Bugs & I continued on our excursions of stealing square lights among other gadgets that Low-rider guys would want to buy.

It was me that started the house burglary stuff and that lead to some pretty fucked up things down the road. Especially after Bugs went away for 7 years for some crazy ass shit him and his older homeboys pulled off. Tony & I were left to fend for ourselves from those that would take advantage of our youth. We fought them off for the most part, but some offers were too tempting to ignore.

But I'm getting ahead of myself here, let me step back a minute and bring you up to speed as to what happened after that dangerous yet exciting night and the events that shaped all of our lives after. We earned some "Stripes" that night. We got some battle wounds and showed we weren't scared of violence. The guys from the neighborhood embraced us as homies from then on. After a short stay in bed Tony resumed his antics on the streets and as our popularity grew, so did our bank account.

By now my dad had started getting sick and wasn't really working anymore. So, I would give my mom money from time to time. It was funny because she asked me once, "mijo, onde garates este dinero?" that was Spanish for where did I get the money from? I simply said "ama, es gratis verda?" she said "si" and I said "tonses no preguntes". She smiled and put it in her pocket. It wasn't much but then again; I was a 11-year-old kid and really didn't have a job that I could speak of. By the time my father died I was well into drugs and shit wasn't going right but all that will come up eventually.

Tony, on the other hand, was having some serious issues with his dad. He didn't approve of Tony bringing stolen bikes to the house or staying out late, hence him locking him out if he wasn't home by 9. Blue was cool, he would sneak a pillow and a blanket out the house and put them in the back of pops truck which had a small camper shell on it. But most times Tony would come to my house or go to Linda's.

One night I was asleep in my parents' room because they had company and I grew up sleeping on a couch (to this day I sleep in one position, never rolling over or if I do I stay in the same place). So, I was in their room and suddenly I hear the window sliding up and looked to see Tony climbing in to wake me up. His dad had locked him out, so he went and stole a van and wanted me to go with him. So, I crept out of bed and peeked out into the kitchen to see what my parents were doing. They were playing cards and having a good time. So, I put my shoes on and slid out the window and off we went.

What happened next was way out crazy and fun. He had parked the van around the corner from my house so he could come get me. But it was also close to where he had stolen the van in the first place. So, by the time we returned to the van, the owner had noticed his van was no longer parked in his driveway, so he had jumped in his truck and was going to go look for it. People did that kind of shit back then. No GPS, no calling the insurance or the cops. Just jump in your other car and drive around and see if you see your shit somewhere.

Well as we were pulling out, guess who pops up behind us? Yes sir! The owner himself, mad as hell too! He pulled up behind us and was just following us when I noticed a truck following us and said to Tony "I think this guy is following us" as Tony sped up, so did the man behind us. But then the chase took an interesting turn when the man decided to try and bump us from behind. For whatever reason I do not know, I promise you. But what I did was, I got up and went to the back of the van as Tony drove around the neighborhood like a madman.

I proceeded to open the back doors of the van and started throwing shit at the truck chasing us. At first it was small stuff like a screwdriver and empty soda cans. But this guy wouldn't give up, so the objects started getting bigger. So here we are hauling ass down the street with this older Mexican man chasing us as I'm throwing shit out the back of the van onto the hood of his truck when we passed a nice police car sitting at the corner.

You know the phrase "There's never a cop around when you need one"? Well, I'm sure that old man would beg to differ, because that cop turned on his little blue cherry on top of his car and gave hot pursuit after us. Cop cars then were white Grand Torino's with a blue rotating light on top, nothing like the cops of today. No tech whatsoever. The man broke off and let the police chase us. I threw some shit at the cop car but that only caused more cops to join in the chase.

Our neighborhood was small in area although it did produce some of San Diego's top hoodlums. A couple of them being these crazy ass Islanders named Pulu and Youngblood. These two guys would not only get chased by the cops on a Yamaha 125 motorcycle, but they would ditch them and as the cop would be sitting at an intersection wondering which way they had gone, here comes Pulu & Youngblood riding a wheelie right in front of the cop's car prompting the cop to give chase again. Sometimes when it was more than one car chasing them, Tony and I would lay in the cut which means we would hide in between parked cars and as soon as Pulu would pass by, we'd rock the cop car. "Us against them" seemed to be the order of the day back then.

As the chase continued, we eventually headed towards the park. There were some city blocks that had been bought out for a freeway project a few years back that never materialized so we had all these vacant lots where many guys would go to park their low-rider's and make out with their girlfriends. Two of these city blocks butted up against the park and brush had overgrown pretty much everything. We would run through them as kids which was cool but as we got older, we found that this was a good place to get away from cops chasing you. The cops really didn't like chasing us in there since they didn't have helicopter coverage because of all the overgrown trees, shrubs, and bushes.

On more than one occasion I busted couples doing the deed in the bushes, of course I dabbled in there myself when the opportunity arose. Anyways, we headed towards the park with a spotlight overhead and 4 or 5 cars behind us. As we drove up this back road towards the park, I returned to my seat to ask what were we going to do? When Tony yells "jump" I looked over to him and saw that he had already jumped out the van and the van was still rolling! I jumped and was dragged for a few feet before I regained my balance and headed towards the bushes. All the while cops were yelling "Freeze!" Yeah, like that was gonna happen.

The moral of that short adventure was that we didn't make money and Tony was upset over it. So, to make up for it about a week later we went back and stole the dudes' truck. The very same truck he had been chasing us in. We hit a small jack pot with that one. We even left some stuff behind after we pillaged the hell out of it. We had parked it in the neighboring city, and we told some friends about it and they went and made out like bandits too, no pun intended.

So it went that we would hit and miss on these missions, but we made out pretty good. We wore new Converse tennis shoes and Pendleton's; these were the things to buy, and it felt good not having to ask moms for money. Although during the black times of my life I would pester the hell out of my moms' about money. Eventually we would go on to Jr. High & later High School. Yet the madness went on.

One-night Bugs and a couple older homies stole a truck and got in a high-speed chase, although they weren't called that back then, and ended up crashing and flipping over with poor Bugs in the back of the truck as it blew up and burned him up pretty badly. Not only that, but he had also been huffing paint, so the flames torched him for the inside too! He lost the ability to speak for a few months and man I used to piss him off to no end because he couldn't yell at me.

He usually just ended up throwing something at me, a wrench, or a pipe. But his teachings never stopped. We learned predictability and how to use it, we learned patience, but most of all we learned stealth. Stealth was something every criminal needs to learn! Stealth will get you in and out of the most dangerous places with your skin still on your body, your bones not broken, but more importantly, your blood in your body. Bugs took us places we never thought possible.

You have to understand we learned quickly because we were young and very impressionable. What I didn't know was that Bugs was teaching us for what was to come later in life if we stayed the course and stay the course, we did no matter what we were confronted with. Whether it was drugs, a woman, or money. Nothing, not even death, would deter us. We stayed the course and focused on what Bugs was teaching us. But in due time I was out smoking PCP and doing some violent shit to other gang members. I know for a fact there are many men out there who wake up every morning and think about the time they fucked up in the wrong neighborhood.

All the while we continued our excursions out into the mean streets of Americas Finest City. I could not understand why it's called that because on our side of town, police regularly would be harassing people; even the good people would get harassed. Then there was this gang unit that rolled around like they were a gang themselves. Always picking on us but in hindsight I am sure we probably deserved it. I mean, think about it, by the age of 12 we were stealing bikes, cars, and anything in your garage that wasn't nailed down. We were fighting our enemies left and right. Burning and tearing shit up. Is what we did and did well.

CHAPTER

The year was 1977 and our little trio took a turn for the worse. 'Bugs' was caught up in some very bad shit that got him sent up to the 'Big House' for 10 years. He eventually did around 7 years and came home but the effect it had on us was too drastic for all concerned. It sounds like we gave up when Bugs left but we didn't. We continued our missions and I got deeper and deeper into the gang scene. Tony had his own car by now; I was still cruising my bike; Linda was still Tonys girlfriend; and the girl I liked finally took notice of me but now she couldn't stand me cause according to her I was an asshole and would continue to be an asshole for the next decade. Never a dull moment in the Barrio.

Once Bugs was out of the picture, some of the older guys of the neighborhood came at us with deals to work for them, do jobs for them. Bugs had always taught us to be wary of such offers because 9 out of 10 times we would get shafted in the deal. But like I said some of these were too good to ignore, so we ventured out and tried them out to see what would come out of it. For instance, one deal was for some friend of a friend that was doing some Union negotiating and this opposition guy was giving them problems.

So here we are a couple of teenagers being sent to rough this guy up. Roughed him up we did too, we sat out in front of dudes house until he got home and just as cool as a cucumber we walked up to him and Tony says "Hey buddy" the guy turns to face him and I crack him in the back of his legs with a baseball bat, he drops to his knees and Tony grabs his face with one hand and gently whispers some nasty shit into his ear and just like that we were gone. We got $100 dollars each, a gram of coke each, and we were happy.

That led to other jobs, but Tony figured out that we could make more on our own. But this is where it gets tricky, some people in this business don't like newcomers coming in and taking business out of their pockets! So, it was hard at first, but we endured the hassle of tough talk from some of these guys like "You better stay out of our business!" I was always like "Or what?" ready to pull out my trusty buck knife and slice into one of these asswipes. They didn't scare me one bit, but Tony was a good businessman (I'll always love him for that). He kept us out of a lot of fights during these times.

Don't misunderstand me for one minute, Tony was a badass through and through, he could chunk'em with the best of them. That's not what I'm getting at. I'm just saying that he had business smarts about him and knew we could make money in these situations if we didn't resort to cracking heads. I myself was just violent as hell and looked for any opportunity to get'em up with someone, the bigger the better too.

I can't emphasize how much my childhood changed after I met Tony. Up until then I had believed in Santa Clause, the Tooth Fairy, La Llorona (a Mexican mythical creature), among other things that normal kids believed in. Don't get me wrong, aside from all the bullshit, I would still wake up early Saturday morning with a big bowl of corn flakes and watch cartoons.

I'm just saying that this guy took me on a journey that a normal adult would have trouble navigating, let alone be successful in it. Only 12 now and set on a life trajectory of heartache, jails, prison, drugs, gangs & death. Oh, add to that a couple kids and one wild ass woman and my life was complete. I started Jr. High with a bang. On the first day of school, I was sent to the principal's office for slamming some guy's face into the lockers. Dude said something about my mom that I did not agree with and as he was walking away, I proceeded to grab his head and smash it into a locker. Of course, that caused a fight between us but most of the fight had already been knocked out of him. I might add that I was part of this new forced bussing program that had started in our fine city by taking kids from the barrios and bussing them to what we referred to as "white boy" schools.

As you can see, I wasn't very fond of the idea and pretty much took it out on this school which I did not want to attend. Rest assured that after being sent to the office on a daily basis and having been suspended as soon as I returned from another suspension that within 2 short months I was kicked out and headed to Gladiator School! A famous school that every young thug aspired to go to, if you didn't go to this school chances where you couldn't bust a grape.

Nestled right smack in the middle of enemy territory this Jr. High school was a proving ground for guys from my neighborhood. Some were made and some were broken. But we went every day for the duration that we were supposed to be there. We used to get chased home like clockwork there. Monday, Wednesdays, & Fridays these vatos would line up and wait for us to walk out of school. We would all group up at the "bench" before & after every class. Then after school, we would begin the stroll down the avenue from 28th street to 32nd street; these vatos wouldn't go past 32nd even though their turf continued all the way to 34th. Reason being was that it was all downhill from there and they did not want to get caught in that little valley that separated our two neighborhoods. So, for the most part we would fight them off as we ran down the street until we'd get to 32nd then we could cruise the rest of the way. We still had to be cautious because it was still enemy territory, they would sometimes but not all the time have some guys waiting down the hill around the corner and we'd have to fight them off too, but it was kind of hairy for them because they still had to get away after and by that time, we had reinforcements coming.

One particular day we had come off a long weekend and on that last day I had got down with one guy that seemed to rub me the wrong way on a daily basis. I had been in class with this dude when we were younger in elementary, but he moved before going on to Jr. High and I hadn't seen him for a minute as I was busy doing other shit and was in another school. Well, this fool ended up joining our enemies' gang and thought he was hot shit so when I saw him, we just would go heads up routinely.

The funny thing though was that he could never best me. Remember I was into karate and loved using that shit. So, on this particular first day of school this fool was waiting outside with about a dozen of his homeboys and like always we would walk right past them, and they would close in on us from behind and start the shit talking. Sometimes we would turn and fight or sometimes we would break and run all depending on who was who in the crowd. This time we were outnumbered but not by many and this idiot was talking mad shit about, "come on Nano" (by usuing my name meant he had serious beef with me) he would chant "One on one" and as I turned back, I see about 6 of them fools unbuttoning their Pendleton's. I say to myself "Yeah right one on one" and continued to walk.

Never put your head down either because that's a sign of weakness. Boom I get smashed in the nose from behind as I'm unbuttoning my shirt and I know this isn't gonna end well. But he strikes first, a little sooner than I had expected but hey it's the law of the jungle. OK I admit he got me good with that one, but I turned around and lit this motherfucker up with a 3 hit combo to the mouth and a stiff kick to the stomach but the kick didn't hurt him as much as I wanted because he had already started backing up. I said "Get some puto, you bad" a phrase that I would use many a time in my years to come.

Well apparently, this quickness I had seemed to knock the wind out of his backups sails because they hesitated to jump in. I was grateful for that because I've been on both the receiving and giving end of those and trust me when I say, "You will feel it tomorrow". So, there he stood bleeding from the mouth jumping up and down like a boxer but wouldn't come near me. I looked back and half of my homeboys were already down the street talking about "Hurry up homes" so I broke out running, fuck it.

Meanwhile on the other side of town, Blue was taking his school studies serious and going to class every day, of course he was a teenager doing teenager shit in school. But Tonys' strictness kind of stuck too so he wasn't as bad as some of the other guys around the neighborhood his age. Remember, I told you him, and I were the same age, so we pretty much ran in the same circles' except when it came time to handle business with Tony. Tony forbid Blue to come anywhere near this shit.

Blue was at another 'white boy' school and he seemed to like it, his charming personality and humorous way to seeing life let him fit in. A couple of other fellas went there too. Some got kicked out, some made their Jr. High & High School careers there, nothing wrong with that. I just felt that I was destined to be in these schools of hard knocks.

Blue had this girl he was fond of, she was homely and cute with a quiet soul, she knew everybody but that's where it ended when it came to her. Blue came into his own there at his school; class clown; stud as a dancer;… man he could shake a leg like no other! Had a charisma about him, almost like Tonys but not quite. By the time his school bus would drop him off in the neighborhood we would already be suited and booted for the evening's shenanigans. Tony would pick me up and off we go to smoke some PCP and go scope out things. Sometimes we would wait till late at night and get dressed all in black and go on missions.

The weekends were for parties. Big head would always throw parties at his moms' house, and they were pretty cool for the most part. Sometimes Tony would see Blue there and send him home; sometimes he would let him stay. Because he would have the hottest chick on the dance floor spinning her like there was no tomorrow. Eventually we'd come to blows with somebody. A party isn't a party until you body slam some stranger in the middle of the street. Now I say eventually because sometimes nobody from other neighborhoods would come, maybe there was a better party elsewhere. So we would end up fighting each other. Let me explain a little here.

At this time, we had two factions in the hood, one was up on the hill, and we were down by the 'tree' which is to say out on the street side of Tonys' mom & dads' house. Right next to the infamous family I mentioned earlier. I say this because one of the brothers would become a dirty rat in the near future, when things went bad for Blue, this piece of shit ended up telling on Blue earning Blue a life sentence (But that's another story). There we would gather and regroup no matter what transpired. Always meet at the 'tree'.

All over the city we would pounce and always come back to the tree. Well like I said, we sometimes would end up fighting each other but by the next day we would be at the park drinking and chilling again as homies. The fights never got too serious between us. Although over personal bullshit some friendships were lost but that's the side, I was talking about that would creep into our souls much later. Little by little we got into selling drugs, man that took us on a crazy ass ride. Now that Bugs was gone, Tony and I would end up doing our thing and looking for any way to make money. We were doing drugs so why not sell them too. In our little part of the world, we shared territory with the blacks.

They had the park, and we would only hang out there but would eventually hang out at the corner store. But as our gang ties grew stronger, we wanted the park, so we went after it. We had mostly been regulated to the back top of the hill part of the park while the blacks had the gym and parking lots of the park. One night some of the boys decided to let off a few rounds over the mayates heads as they were playing basketball. That cleared out the park for the rest of the night. It was also the beginning of the end for them controlling the park. After a couple nights of this we eventually walked down the hill right into the gymnasium and let these people know it was our park now. It was rather easy for some reason because they didn't put up any resistance whatsoever. Don't misunderstand me here, the park was still open to the blacks, only now we controlled it. I mean we aren't animals after all.

We just saw it as good business to control the land we were selling drugs on. The main drug on the streets then was PCP, 'wet daddies' as we would refer to them back then. I have to say that this drug made and broke a lot of fools back then. Some got high and never came back down, I was very fortunate because I smoked so much of this stuff that I nearly lost my mind 2 or 3 times a week. But for some reason I managed to keep my faculties about me, and now I sit here and am able to tell my story. Back to business, Tony found a connection for the PCP and off we went selling enough drugs to get high for free. Although the number one rule in dope selling is as everyone knows that "You don't get high on your own supply" but we've been against all odds up until this point, so why change now?

So, as you might have guessed, got high on our own supply we did! We smoked so much that my boy was sometimes referred to as "Dipstick". We smoked that shit early in the morning before school and first thing out of school, during karate lessons, we sometimes would get so bombed we'd forget where we were and just end up parked somewhere randomly.

But Tony managed to make money and keep us high as fuck all summer long. The dope selling game was a crowded game, blacks, and other gangs were selling this shit. Territories were being fought for. Robberies were the norm around these parts. It seemed like whoever was more determined to have the cash was willing to go to war over this shit. The boys from the Hill made out like bandits on their side of town even though they were trafficking on the same turf as the blacks.

CHAPTER

Meanwhile back at home my father had fallen ill, from his drinking. Don't get me wrong, my father was a good and decent man, he provided for his family and was always there to give advice or yell at us when we messed up at home and to be honest, I was happy that he was my dad, I really tried to be a good boy for him. I was very respectful to him and would never try and come home high so he could see me (can't say that about my brothers). My brothers although were nowhere near the shit I was into, they smoked weed and even though it was illegal back then, it wasn't as bad as PCP. No, I really believe if my father saw the shit I was into out in the streets he would have beat the living crap out of me. He eventually caught on to some of my street madness but by then it was too late. I was a fully-fledged gang member and addicted to PCP so the most he did was talk to me. That conversation went over very smooth. I learned from it and even gave my own son the same advice when his time came, the roles had been reversed and I was the father.

One night I was at the park with some older homeboys, and I had a brand-new felt-tip marker and starting writing on the pole when one of the older guys grabbed the marker out of my hands (of course he was a little drunk, so I didn't argue with him). He started writing on the pole but was being a little aggressive with the marker and I said, "Hey man be cool" and he smashed the marker full force into the pole ruining my brand-new marker. So, I pushed him, and he socked me!

I turned around and started walking away, when one of the homies started following me, he came up behind me and said "What you gonna do homes? You got that walk". So, I told him "I'm gonna get this fool" so he said he was going to go with me just to see what I do.

Fucking weirdo if you ask me, so off we went to my house. When we got there, I sneaked into my parents' room. I knew my dad had guns I knew one was a legit gun and one was a throw away. I grabbed the throw away and stuffed it in my pants. The whole time this knucklehead was outside waiting for me. So, I walk back out and tell him "Let's go" and off we go back to the park.

Once we got there, I approached the group and yelled at the older homeboy "Fuck with me now!" and that caught everyone's attention. But nobody was really responding until I pulled out the gun and pointed it at the guy I was gunning for. He was kind of sitting on a small patch of grass next to the pole we had been writing on. At that moment everybody seemed to move away from him and kind of stood to the side. He said "quit fucking around" to which I responded by firing a shot into the ground right next to him and watched the dirt splash upwards like a small wave crashing on a rock. Some even landed on him as he leaned over to one side. I know it scared him because he most likely didn't think I would do that. "You think I'm playing" I answered.

By now his brother was creeping up on me from the side and I caught him through my peripheral vision. So, I turned the gun on him and said, "I'll kill you too!" that pretty much stopped him dead in his tracks. I told him "Get over there with your brother" then I had another thought and yelled at the rest of the fellas there to get under the light. I made the older homie get up and slowly walk over to me. As he approached me with his hands up, I pointed the gun right at his forehead, and said "you my older homie and I respect you, but don't you ever fuck with me like that again". He readily agreed and I turned and walked away. I didn't want to shoot the guy, he was my homeboy after all, but I had to show this fool that even though I was a youngster I was not to be trifled with.

For the next 40 years, me and that homie got along for the most part. Can't say the same for his brother though. Him and I got into blows a few times, at the park, in the street. But eventually the knowledge that his brother learned was learned by him as well. Oh, I did get into one fist fight with my older homie since that night, we were at a party years down the road and he saw me talking to his girlfriend and accused me of trying to get with her (she was like a foot taller than me). Drunk and jealous people will let their minds really fuck with them.

The night I used my dad's throw away gun I went home and put it back without getting caught, or so I thought. A couple days after that night at the park I came home to eat dinner and my dad was in the living room watching TV. I entered and greeted my dad with a peek on the cheek and he said in Spanish "I want to talk to you" so I said "sure" but that I had to go pee first. He said OK so I went to the restroom and drained the 'lizard', washed my hands after, walked back to the living room and sat down on the couch next to my father. "What's up dad?" I said in Spanish, I think I should let you know that in my father's house one could not speak English. We were not allowed to speak to him in English which is cool because he wanted us to be able to speak Spanish. It worked too because I do, fluently.

He said in a serious voice "not here, outside" which really tripped me out because he had never spoken to me in such a voice and it kind of scared me. But being the little thug/gangster/thief/conniver that I was I immediately started thinking of the shit that I've done that could cause harm to my family! So, I got up and walked outside with him. It felt eerily walking behind him because I wasn't a stranger to walking behind someone and not knowing the outcome of what was about to transpire. But this was my father and to him I was his 'Papi" as he would call me. We walked out onto the porch, and he motioned for us to go down the stairs.

So, I followed him down but man I gotta say that up until this very moment I had been involved in a shitload of shit. But none that could follow me home. As far as my home life went, I was an average kid, I went to school every day, not to class but to school, I was doing my karate everyday (I got a whole section on that crazy adventure). I did my chores at home like I was supposed to.

The only bad thing was I had a bike made out of stolen parts at home but that was it. Respect for my mom and dad kept me from coming home high or bringing any of the street bullshit home. So, I was wondering what in God's name could I have done that could jeopardize the house? We got to the bottom of the stairs and what my dad said next really blew my fucking mind. He said (again in Spanish), "I brought you out here because I didn't want your mother to hear". OK that was it! I was about ready to come clean on anything he would have accused me of or insinuated I might have been a part of. He continued "Obviously whatever you did, you got away with" I'm sitting there stone cold faced and quickly slipping into my mode because honestly I had forgotten about the gun. I had no idea what he was talking about. You have to understand that I'm an up-and-coming thug not really knowing what is in store for me on this path that I was walking. The thing with the gun was done in anger and I wasn't really thinking because I let pride get to me. So, after I did it, I went on with my other shenanigans.

Then my dad says that I'm not a kid no more and that I clearly know the difference between right and wrong. That he was no longer going to treat or talk to me as a kid. I now am old enough to make my own decisions. "But and I put emphasis on the 'But,' if you get caught doing something wrong, don't come crying to me!" This conversation was a turning point for me. It let me know that pops was no fool and that he could be cool too.

"If you gonna use my gun son replace the bullets" he said to me. It was so awesome that the part of knowing the difference between right and wrong really got to me that I said to myself "one day I'll say this to my son". Only when it came time for me to say it to my son, I didn't say it quite as eloquently as my father had said it to me. I was more like "OK motherfucker, you know the difference between right and wrong. So, you gonna make your decisions, but I tell you right now, get caught doing something wrong and your ass better not call me." But I was blessed in that my son turned out not to be a terrorist like I had turned out.

And so it went that while Tony and I continued our missions, almost on a nightly basis, we would target cars and houses and go in and do some damage and people would wake up in the morning and be like "oh damn, honey somebody broke into your car". Time and time again we would wander other areas of town because by now we had learned that you don't steal from your own back yard. But I have to admit that every once in a blue moon I would be so high that I would just say "fuck it" and smash right there in the hood. I wouldn't care in the morning as long as I got away.

One night Tony and I partied with a couple of my karate school buddies, Benny & Sal; we ended up going on a rampage in my neighborhood. We went from street to street literally running from car to car breaking in them and just taking small shit, enough to say we took something. It got to the point that me and one of my friends, 'karate Ben' sat down on a small wall by the park and watched these 2 other fools running up and down the street and eventually we saw the smoke billowing from the other block and these two knuckleheads came back. They had set fire to a camper on back of some one's truck.

At home my dad was steadily going in and out of the hospital. He was very sick. I loved my dad with all my heart because he had such high hopes for me if and when I grew up. I remember once he was in the hospital, and I had left town on a karate trip. I went to fight in a tournament in Fresno. My instructor didn't go with us on this trip. Instead, the next highest-ranking dude was in charge, he was a Brown Belt. Our group also had a Purple Belt, Blue Belt, Green Belt, and my little ass with an Orange Belt. Needless to say, that we kicked ass over there up in Fresno, CA came back with 17 trophies we did including Black belt Grand Champion.

We came back home and since there were no pagers, cell phones, or Facebook back then we all said our goodbyes at the studio and went our separate ways. The head of the school was later notified about the great job his students had done at this tournament especially the Black Belt. Needless to say, the instructor was shocked because he didn't send any Black Belts. But he gave us props.

The very next day I took one of the trophies I won in that tournament to visit my dad in the hospital. I carried it in a brown grocery bag, walked in his room and he was happy to see me. Then I opened the bag and pulled it out and said "miar Apa, lo que te gane" he got really happy and sure as shit he got better and came home in a couple days. He was really proud of my fighting abilities, although he really wanted me to be a boxer. I was like "fuck that, you get hit in the head too much". At least with karate I could kick a fool back.

Now my personal instructor who was in charge of the Jr. Team was a way the fuck out character. He was young and one bad ass kick boxing fool. This dude had over 700 trophies in his room. I remember walking in the first time and seeing all he had was trophies and a desk in there. It was cool and weird at the same time.

Cool because I wanted that many trophies in my room but that wasn't in the cards for me with this karate thing. Turns out my instructor was a drug dealer with a lot of enemies. He played on a much higher level than me and Tony was playing on. But he had found out one way or another that aside from taking karate I was a little hoodlum. So, he figured he could use me in more ways than just fighting in tournaments representing our school.

He brought me to his house one night and asked if I wanted to smoke some 'wack'(PCP). Now I don't know if he was testing me or what because he was my karate instructor. He was teaching me self-discipline and how to take care of my body and to kick ass of course but that's not the point here; the point here is that after he offered me some dope to smoke. It was safe to say after this that our friendship was irrecoverably changed forever. OK so we got high together for the first time but not the last and remember I said this was a crazy adventure. This man started taking me on spying missions. He would have me sit outside somebody's house until they went to sleep. I would creep up to the bedroom window and tape a huge M–80 onto it. Light the Fuse and run down the street to see what happens. Boom the firecracker would blow, scaring the living shit out of whoever was inside. He never told me whose house it was or why I did it. Then after a couple of other missions my karate lessons became free, fuck the dumb shit. We even started partying together with a couple of other people associated with the karate school. We'd go rent a hotel room and while me and the other guys were in the room getting high, this motherfucker was in the restroom making up ounces of 'Angel Dust" for delivery. He would come out of the restroom with a brief case and hand it to one of us with a piece of paper with an address on it, off we'd go to deliver this large amount of PCP for distribution in our fine city. Man, this guy was ruthless, here he had kids who were trained to kick ass and loyal as fuck to him, delivering drugs to smaller dealers for him.

Don't misunderstand me, we were delivering to the dealer's dealer. We never saw any street dealers or never went to a bad side of town. Like I said this cat was playing on a higher level. But either way, add this shit to the crazy adventures I had with Tony and my street gang shenanigans, and my life was pretty full. '78' and '79' rolled by like the blink of an eye.

My father died when I was in the 9th grade. Although he had stopped drinking, I believe the damage had been done to his body and it finally just took him. Threw me for a loop! I would get into fights at school and that would land me in trouble or the fact that I had a mouth like a full-grown sailor drunk on the waterfront mad at his wife for cheating on him! I ended up on probation and my Probation Officer would tell my mom that I was dumb and got caught doing dumb stuff. She had no idea about the shit I was into.

My probation officer was a lady that was kind of cool, an attractive lady (for a copper) but still did her job. She would try and creep up on me at home but like I was cool at home, so she never got anything. She once saw me at the little park down the street from my house and saw me with a couple of fellas and stopped. So, I walked over to her car, and she asked what I was doing there. I told her I was coming home from school, so she offered a ride. I accepted because I didn't want her messing with my homies. I was carrying this huge boom box, but they were called 'Ghetto Blasters" back then. I got in her car, and she asked where did I get that from? So, I just said it belonged to a friend. Little did she know that I had jacked some dude for it after cracking his ass with a stick a few times.

She was a nice lady but a hell of a naïve person. I didn't push her, and I acted like the kid she thought I was as long as it kept me out of juvenile hall. You see even though cops and probation people are in touch with each other the cops see one side and the probation sees another.

So, my Probation Officer saw what went on at home with me. By this time, I was well known to the cops in my area. This damn Gang Unit, they really hated Tony and since I was Tony's right-hand man they just naturally came after me too. Tony by now was way ahead of them. He was living away from the hood with some chick he met in school while he still attended. His true love Linda was pregnant with his baby and still living in the hood. Shit was getting deep for us, newly formed gangs were trying to make a name for them-selves and as we were way ahead in the game, it was natural that they tried to hit us.

Gangs are funny that way. We went after the bigger gangs because we were relatively small for the bullshit we signed up for, and some of the larger older gangs came after us but it seemed luck, skill, and balls were on our side because we fought these fools like there was no tomorrow! If you stop to think about it, it could have been anyone of us there would be no tomorrow for.

CHAPTER

Blue was doing his thing. He had become well known in the neighborhood as a young ladies' man, knew how to get a party started and was a charismatic leader for the youth at school. His relationship with Tony was as strong as ever but their father was really hating on Tony, after kicking him out and not really wanting anything to do with him. Causing friction between Pops and Blue but Blue was strong, he didn't let his father's anger towards Tony get him down too much. He loved his father too. Tony, although not really dressing like a gang member did, was one hell of a gang leader. He had a small band of radical youngsters following him that would do anything he said. He really won everyone over when one night at a party the boys from the up the Hill were having and were refusing to let our guys in!

As the guy at the gate was telling everyone they couldn't get in Tony arrived and pushed his way through the crowd grabbed o'l boy by the shoulder swung him around and punched him in the jaw, knocking him out cold. He then told all the fellas from the Tree "let's go to our side, there's a party over there" so everyone just followed him off. I was doing a 3 month stretch for refusing to snitch on my homies little brother who had given my little cousin a stolen bike and I got caught on it. I heard about this event through a letter I received from my homegirl who wrote to me on a weekly basis because that's what homegirls do for their homeboys when they are locked up.

So, everybody went to the party on "our side" of town. When the homie who Tony had knocked out finally woke up, he asked "who the fuck was that?" This certain homie was a bit older and had just got out of prison, so he knew but didn't know. He was told that it was Tony and after shaking it off he gathered some fellas of his own and headed to our side of town!

Mad as hell too he was. The party at this girl's house was in full bloom with people on the dance floor, fellas gathered around the keg of ice-cold beer, music bumping the tunes of the day. By now the Stylistics, Blue Magic, and Marvin Gaye had moved over for the new and funky sound of Rick James, Lakeside, & Cameo. Although the sound of the mid 70's will live forever, room had to be made for the new sounds.

In walked the fellas from the Hill and as everyone had expected he stood at the doorway and shouted for Tony, "me and you motherfucker one on one!" The dance floor cleared, and these 2 titans met in the middle and even though I wasn't there to see it, those who were there said it was the fight of the century! These two fools went toe to toe (Calling someone a fool doesn't necessarily mean they are foolish; it just means they are zip damn fools). They locked horns right there in the middle of the dance floor. Mostly landing face shots one after the other they pounded each other until what seemed like an eternity but was probably only a minute. Then they stopped and drank a beer after. The fight I assume was symbolic for what was to transpire after.

I eventually got out. The year was 1981; drugs were being sold, smoked and the older guys shot it up their veins. I could never understand that principal of sticking a needle in one's arm. But it is what it is, people will do whatever it is they fall into in their lives. I, for one, was a sherm-head which is to say I smoked PCP until I could smoke no more. I out smoked the best of them. It took me down a dark road that really affected many people around me.

Tony was in a dark place himself; he had made some serious enemies doing what he was doing. His enemies were my enemies. We had stolen cars from black people, broke into homes we weren't supposed to fuck with, we were selling drugs on other people's territory but one thing he did that was really over the top was he had stolen some money that I never really knew where he got it from. I did know it was a lot and that he had buried it somewhere in the neighborhood. One day he called me on the phone at home and told me to meet him at the tree. So off I go to the tree, and he swung by and picked me up. "Get in" he said, and I jumped in his car, and we cruised around for a little while talking but eventually we stopped to smoke a "stick" PCP came in different forms then and had many different names.

We parked in this vacant lot we had named 'Baldemar's Park'. It wasn't a real park just a vacant lot but the old men from the neighborhood used to sit in chairs there and drink their beer. They would play a game that I never understood. Maybe it was from the old country but still that's what we named this place. As we sat in the car, he started telling me about our situation in this vicious game we'd been playing and where and how we stood in the eyes of the underworld. We talked about upcoming jobs and meetings we would have with other drug dealers.

Then he dropped it on me. I'm sure that by now you understand this man and I were very close; we had been running together since we met almost on a daily basis (other than the times we did in Juvenile Hall). We had been through some pretty harrowing situations; we held strong when we lost Bugs to the 'Big House', we had even gotten into a fist fight with each other. I trusted him and he trusted me without question. He said to me "If I'm gone, look out for my brother" taken aback a bit I asked, "where you going?" he answered "nowhere, I'm just saying look out for my brother" but I continued "why? Where you going?" then he says "look, my brother don't listen to me he listens to you. I'm his brother you're his homeboy. I don't want this bullshit for him, just look out for him!" "OK".

"I want to tell you where the money is buried" I'm like "Why?" then I ask again "Where the fuck are you going" he tells me again that he isn't going anywhere but I'm really tripping out because we are young and pretty stable in our little world. Yes, we sometimes bended or ignored the rules of the underworld but we never hurt the wrong people. The only people we really hurt were our families at home, but we were so blinded by ambition, money, and glory, or so we thought. I never once thought that this very world that we strived to be a part of would tire of us and not want us. But there was something Tony would not tell me. So, for the sake of argument, I agreed to what Tony was asking of me, but I was adamant about him not telling me where the money was buried. Instead, I insisted that if he was going to tell someone it should be his father. He and his father were rarely speaking at this point in time. So, in the long run I believe he did tell his father.

Later that month we had set up a meeting with this dude that worked at a mortuary close by and had access to the main ingredient for PCP. We had worked a deal for a 5-gallon drum of the stuff in exchange for a percentage of the money we would generate from the sales in street value. Instead, what happened is we met at the park and while we waited a group of unknown assailants attacked our group and, in the end, Tony was dead! Killed for reasons known or unknown, we never found out who it was or why it happened.

All I knew was that my best friend, my brother was dead! I sustained a blow to the head and didn't remember or saw anything. When I awoke, we took Tony to the hospital but I'm pretty sure his wounds had already killed him. I was detained for a couple hours but released in the wee hours of the morning. I went home and cried because I didn't know what else to do. Someone had notified Tonys' family of what had happened because when I got there later that morning Blue came out into the yard and sat on the couch we had back there and as he wept, I knelt at his feet without saying a word.

The cops didn't give a shit about Tonys' death although they put up a good front about it. They acted like they investigated it, but nothing ever came out of it. It was a bad day for the neighborhood. He was only 19 years of age when he died. So young, what kind of grown man he would have been would never be realized. Can't even say he was cut down in his prime, the man wasn't even halfway through his young adult life.

He died on a Monday night, and we buried him a week later. The neighborhood turned out in full force to pay their final respects to the guy who had put us on the map. The funeral itself was a very sad and solemn event. For all of us who had had a close relationship with him were heart-broken by this loss. This young man was the one who set the rules for our side of town which have remained in effect to this day and introduced us to a way of life that one could only see in movies.

What motivated him no one knew? What we did know was that he set for us a way to survive in this world we lived in. I should have learned but I didn't. I lost my mother-fucken mind right about then! Losing Bugs was one thing because with that I had bragging rights to say I knew him and that he will be back but losing my dad and now Tony was a little too much for my young brain and heart to handle. I fell into this drug induced dream of sorts. No one was as affected by this loss more than I, other than Blue. I stopped going to school, I stopped doing my karate, and I did way more drugs than anyone around me. Life sucked for me at this point in time. I was 16 years old and had my whole life in front of me. I could have turned over a new leaf and gone straight.

But instead, I chose to go deep into this dark place that only a few venture into and come back from. I was high from morning till night and would not eat or sleep much. I didn't care about anything or anyone. My family was struggling with their own problems with the death of my father as I was, but I was also dealing with the death of my best friend! Tony was my inspiration in this world, as I was his right hand in all he did. Something had drawn us together in this world something had put him in my path to show me how to deal with life on this side of the world. What we were involved in was against societies rules but society didn't give a fuck about us, so we learned how to live this way. It still wasn't fair; this much pain for one young kid was too much for me to bear.

I slipped into the dark easily. Blue was handling it better than I was. At least he stayed home and tried his best to comfort his mom while his dad dealt with it in his own way. For the time being at least it seemed like he would be OK. But seeing what he saw and hearing what he heard led him outside to the bad side of things, and his journey to the dark side enveloped him a lot quicker than it did me.

For starters, he had relatives from that crazy-ass city to the north of us, the big Barrio known as East LA. They had come down one day and gave Blue a gun and said, "Handle it". Blue did just that, he

'Handled it' without fear or any such thought which would have or might have persuaded him not to. He went on a frenzied drug induced wild rampage that left one dead and many, many others tore up in its' wake. Blue wouldn't listen to me or anyone for that matter, I don't think he could have if he wanted too. He was tormented by his one and only brother's death, blinded by pure anger and need for vengeance! He just let the darkness take him, he accepted it wholeheartedly, and with a feverish passion he drove himself to the point of no return! Before anyone knew, he was slammed down in Juvenile Hall on a minor law infraction.

Sitting out his 30-day sentence he started to think clearly, and he remembered bits and pieces of the last month or two of what had transpired. He really didn't know how he would deal with the rest of his life. Or anything for that matter. In the meantime, I was busy doing my own set of drugs, in a haze and looking for any type of solution that would bring me some kind of peace. But it seemed that peace was something far from my or any of us' reach at this point in time.

We, although not in touch with one another, were still bound to each other through the gang bond, continued on our banging ways. Bringing as much pain to the other street gangs of our day, we roamed the city night and day looking for enemy combatants. I myself was becoming quite famous for doing so much drugs and still being able to bang on our enemies. I had no idea who, what, where or when I did what I did. I was so far gone into the dark that I let go of all responsibilities I had worked so hard to gain. My mind was a constant blur as days passed without time or anything relating to it.

My health wasn't as great as it was when Bugs had us in training. But I believe that that's what kept me alive through these difficult days. I wasn't eating much so my weight dropped to skin and bones. My clothes were in shambles, even though I had taken to dressing rather sharp during my profitable days. But the loss that I was going through took the steam right out of me and I just didn't care if I was coming or going. Other people around the neighborhood were just as shocked as I was over the death of 'TonyRich' but most of them handled it a lot better than I. Some continued with school until they graduated and got the hell out of there! Joined the service or went to college, anything to get away from the neighborhood. But I was so far gone that even my family was starting to give up on me except for my mother and that meant a lot to me although I didn't know it right then until much, much later.

Remember I said I would bother her a lot about money later on, well this is the time that I would lie, beg, or steal from her. She defended me to everyone else in the family. They all said she should kick me out or call the cops (yeah, like she would really do that to me). Slowly I slipped into the darkness and to be honest I welcomed it because at least while I was high the pain in my heart gave way to hatred and vengeance and that didn't hurt at all. The days, the weeks, months, and years flew by like the wind. It was then that I started going in and out of jail, like it was the thing to do.

Blue ended up fighting a murder case in Juvenile Hall, I believe he came to terms about everything because he said to me in a letter "Fuck it homes I'm gonna do 20 calendars in here" but in the end he stayed forever. Remember I mentioned this infamous family? Well, it turns out Blue was with this piece of shit that fateful night and to save his own ass this punk decided to tell, snitch, and rat on Blue. This piece of shits entire family became outcasts in the neighborhood, nobody would have anything to do with them. No harm ever came to them. An unspoken rule was that they didn't do anything! It was their brother that was the rat, and he was the one with a price on his head. Eventually they moved away.

Funny thing about jail though. In there, the only enemies we had were the blacks and whites. No Mexicans fought against each other! It was strange for me the first trip to the county jail. In Juvenile Hall we still gang banged but not so much in the county. I was thrust into this 'High Power' tank (that's what they call holding cells for really bad crimes). Because of my crimes and I stood alone in a corner watching as they would bring inmates in and out. I would really trip out on how dudes from one neighborhood would be all chummy with dudes from another neighborhood. I was taught that if you 'ain't from the neighborhood' we ain't friends.

Then one day as lunch was being served, an older vato sitting next to me noticed my last name on my wristband and let me know he went to school with some dude with that same name. Turns out he went to school with one of my older brothers. This cat had been in the system a good taste of time and saw my apprehension. He asked if it was my first time here, to which I said yes, and he asked if I was active in the gang banging scene. Again, I said yes, he then proceeded to explain that in the county, us gang members had to leave that type of thinking at the door.

Even though this cat was hella cool I still followed my own set of rules. I refused to get chummy with any of them and then I saw one dude from my days in juvenile hall, Louie from down south. We weren't friends by far, but we recognized one another and started talking. Since we were youngsters, we were regulated to our own bench and as we watched these older Fools shaking hands and letting each other know who was where and what kind of case they were fighting. I said to Louie "That's gonna be us in 10 years" and he agreed.

Meanwhile the madness continued on the "outs" as we so fondly called it. My neighborhood had gone to war with 2 gangs to the east simultaneously which was a pretty bad one. It lasted a couple years and cost a few lives on both sides. To this day I hate those fuckers, but life goes on. In the end I buried a lot of homeboys over this 'Vida Loka' shit. Saw a lot of families broken over this bullshit. We were blamed for many deaths in our neighborhood, it was our fault someone lost a brother or son, and maybe it was. We did a lot of fucked up shit in those days. Never really caring who we hurt and what not. It's cool I don't blame them for feeling that way.

It was around this time, in 1981 or 1982, I was out on the streets still getting high but had it a little better under control. I met this girl. I have to admit that I first saw this dame at a concert and what I saw really caught my eye. She was short, thick, and sexy as fuck. But no matter what I tried that night she kept shooting me down, talk about crash & burn, I went down in flames, but I think I got to her too. So, a couple months after that encounter I met her again and this time she was more receptive to my charm, a charm I didn't know I had but it seemed to work. We snuck off to "talk" but ended up in the back seat of her car. This went on for about 2 months before she dropped a bomb on me.

She said her parents wanted to "meet" me. As if I didn't have enough crap going on in my life. She was persistent, I give her that. Before I go on, I have to tell you that she is "white" and from the other side of the tracks. I didn't say the wrong side I just said the other side. Well, it went down like this, it was a Friday night, and I washed my car that belonged to my mom but was mine for the night, took a shower, and put on some clean clothes. Keeping in mind that I was a fully-fledged gang member and dressed the part of one to a T.

I looked very dapper for a young thug of the day if I do say so myself. Alas, my little bubble of coolness was to be popped as soon as I drove to her semi-affluent neighborhood. I swear if they had cell phones and FaceBook back then, I would have gone viral "Young Mexican Gang Member Walking around White Neighborhood", but in the end it was well worth it. She put up with my shit for 8 years and blessed me with 2 young'uns. But at the end of 8 years, she took the kids and ran. I can't say that I blame her much, I really was quite the fucked-up boyfriend. I didn't pay attention to her, I just wanted to get high and cause havoc to my enemies. I believe she was ready to settle down as she had gone through her own set of issues on her side of town with her parents.

I mean come on here she was a very beautiful well off-white girl living in a big house with a halfway decent future ahead of her and she decides to take up with the likes of me! From the very first meeting I was hated with a vengeance. I was the guy mothers warned their daughters about, and here I was in the flesh at their home. I tried to be cool at first, but they were just like anybody else that wasn't from the neighborhood, 'Fuck'em'. So, our rocky relationship came to an abrupt end around 1989. I was in prison on some stupid drug charges, and she was looking for love elsewhere, but life is such.

Nothing I could do but go on with what I knew. I did my little time standing on my head, cleared my mind of just about everything that was in there, and rebuilt my body health wise. I exercised every day and brought myself back out of the hole I had put my soul into after Tony got killed. A wild ass ride for any young person to endure but endured it I did and now my release date was fast approaching from this rat-ass joint I was being housed in. I set my mind to what awaited me on the outs. To take back what was rightfully mine.

CHAPTER

The 90's were a truly happening time for us in the neighborhood. Don't get me wrong. Death, prison, drugs, and ass kicking's were still there just waiting to pounce on one of us like a panther pouncing on its prey. But this time around would be different for me most of all. I had taken the last couple of years to really go over what had happened to us, by us, for us. My mind was set, and I was determined to stay ahead of the game that Tony and I had started so long ago.

The foundation that Tony had laid for us was still there, the people that gave us support were still there although we did lose Bugs to a senseless shooting while I was still away. I was saddened by his passing almost as much as Tonys' death, but the times were changing, and I had to stay focused as Bugs had taught us. Stay the course was one of our mottos as kids, it would be so now as a grown ass man!

I was released during the winter of '91' and no one saw me coming. I hit the streets quietly. But try as I might my return to the neighborhood was not to be secret. As soon as one knuckle head found out I was back in town the word spread like wildfire, which I could really have done without because it also alerted my enemies and those that had done wrong in my absence. Either way I was primed for battle in any way, shape, or form.

I had come to reclaim what was mine and had a plan to do it. Yes of course there was a list, people and things that need to be handled. One by one they fell to broken jaws or broken knees. My claim to the turf was in full swing by the beginning of the summer. I had re-established my crew and set up shop all over the town. There was still some resistance but nothing to get in a twist about. They would succumb to my rule eventually.

A youngster from the neighborhood known as "Blanks" came to me in early '92' with an idea. He was very young but quite ambitious for his age. Didn't quite remind me of me. He was more intense, more focused on his goal or plan. Whatever it was this kid was ready. We went in on a buy together and started doing business together. He was more disciplined than I when it came to money because I was into spending money on dates, food, or bullshit. For starters I even had a Limousine driver on call just so we could go to dinner. This kid Blanks had restraint on his side. Of course, he spent also but just not as carelessly as I would. He was so adjusted and strict that it scared me at times.

Once we were in LA on some business. He was in the house as I waited outside with one order: to come in blasting if he wasn't out in 20 minutes. Thinking it was cool, I called a girl on the car phone and was throwing some lines in her direction to see if I could get any playtime with her when all of a sudden, the door opens and in jumps Blanks. This young man was livid with me. Of course, he respected me as an older homie from the hood but as he put it so bluntly: "This is business!" Yes, I understood that there were guys looking to rob us or kill us and then there were the guys from the south that we represented that would not find it humorous at all if anything like that were to happen to us or to their shipment for that matter. We weren't as concerned about the heat as we were about these other elements in this game because the heat played by rules and these other fools were fucking ruthless. Blanks was not about to let me forget this or let this shit happen again.

I'm getting ahead myself again, let me back up a bit and tell you how we started and the simple idea or concept that Blanks had for us. In our area there were a few dealers, some worked together, some were independent. Independents didn't last long: because they were independent, they were able to navigate anywhere in the city. Don't get me wrong, if I wanted to do that, I could have but I was gang affiliated so I was bound by Gang Law. Independents had no structure and dealt with anybody, anywhere. Which left them open to taxers taxing the hell out of them, they had no one to answer to who could intervene for them when something of this nature happened. Believe me when I say I saw some fucked up shit befall these free- sprit mother'fuckers.

Now the dealers that worked together had it easier, or less expensive. They would talk to one another make sure they didn't over-step each other's boundaries. These were the guys we dealt with to start off with a simple 100-dollar investment. Within months we were into QP's and steadily moving our way up to PD's. Blanks idea was to become the supplier to the dealers. Especially: the dealer supplying us. Also keep it as quiet as we can. So it came to pass that after many, many drug deals we became an entity of sorts in the underworld of drugs.

Blanks, was a serious character in this game. He was loyal to only a few and was very strict in his dealing of treatment of those that opposed his business policies. Always one to check the inner workings of his empire he once purposely disappeared on me for a week & I couldn't find his young ass any-where. Pissed me off to no end that I had to go outside for a buy to keep the business running. Doing stuff like that wasn't my idea of fun but money has a funny way of coming or going and one has to deal with this beast from time to time. It was Supply & Demand.

Eventually the youngster arrives a week later fresh out the shower and simply asks me "what you been up to?" man I was like "You weren't around so I went outside to keep the business running!" He seemed satisfied with that answer with the remark "So you kept the ball rolling?" A troubling thought this was. Here I am a General to troops of sorts and this high school kid had just tested me to see what I would do in a circumstance of his choosing. To be both mad and flattered was kind of cool and it gave me a new respect for this youngster.

We entered into an agreement, to be loyal, and true to our game. He understood that I was bound by Gang Law and I would not touch certain areas of this game, Without divulging anything, Blanks was ok with that and he would address these areas and situations as they came up. We once had to deal with another dealer, but he belonged to another local gang, so I would not deal with him (even though later on we became friends). I would not do any business with him. This is akin to 'consorting with the enemy' which is a serious crime in my neighborhood. And other parts of the world, I'm sure. I wasn't aware of the rest of the world back then because my Barrio was my world. Nothing else mattered, nor should it if one is in this type of game that can end in long stints in jail or planted in a cemetery.

Like I said we started out small with a hundred bucks dealing nickels & dimes. I was also moonlighting as a bodyguard for one of the neighborhood dealers. He was big-time but no one in the neighborhood knew. He never dealt in the neighborhood, he lived there and even had a job, but his business dealings were with people from other parts of the city, some I didn't even know. I just knew this fella was making big dollars. As he grew, he needed someone to watch his property in the hood and seeing as I was having trouble at home, he liked the idea of me staying in his garage/office/storage/man cave. He also had a house and a couple of apartments on the property to which I made sure stayed safe in his absence. He was a cool dude until he did me wrong.

We went our separate ways but not before I took him for a couple piles of money. Gang Law demanded it, and who was I to ignore Gang Law? He thought he could overcome my idle threats, but when I put a strap to his head and made him agree to pay for his sins, all went my way. On the other hand, he eventually was making so much money the people running half the state stepped in and cut his profits short. Last I heard of him he was driving a truck for a living.

I had my crew of loyal people; we had the neighborhood tight. The merger with Blanks and his crew was a beneficial move for both of us. He saw the power & muscle I had, and I saw the business talent he had. It was a simple solution to this equation. Merge and watch what happens. Of course, we discussed many things in the process and had disagreements, but we saw eye to eye and things worked out fine.

Blanks was into other stuff other than just dealing drugs. He was 17 and in high school, but man this kid was on his toes. He went to school during the day and had a thieving crew at night (I myself had stopped my thieving ways a few years back when I realized I made more money doing the dope game). They would jack mini trucks and take rims and stereo systems. They weren't like Tony, Bugs & me. These fuckers had 2-way radios for crying out loud. They had lookouts and code names. It was a sight to see.

He even had a contract with some people down south, he was taking motorcycles and jet-skis to them for some resort they had on some exotic beach. These were grown ass men and thought they could take advantage of this kid. I don't remember the story well, but they told him to meet them at some grocery store parking lot and supposedly were going to pay him. He didn't like the feeling he was getting and ran it down to me and asked if I would go with him.

We drove to this parking lot and strategically parked the car, so they wouldn't see us. They knew what kind of car he drove, so we were at a disadvantage because we didn't know theirs. Eventually they pulled up on my side of the car so I'm facing the passenger side of their car which was the dudes muscle guy like I was Blanks muscle.

They seemed a bit surprised that he would show up with an older gang member as muscle because the weird smile they had of their face quickly disappeared when they saw my face. A look that I've perfected over the years; it's been said that I never smile. It let them know I wasn't here to bullshit. I was also quick to show them the two 9 mm handguns that sat in my lap. They paid him and continued to do business with him, but we never took them up on their offer of going down to their resort for a free vacation.

There's a saying in my neighborhood, "Momma didn't raise no fool." We were sure to keep things on a good note and not cross the wrong people or if it happened be prepared for any and all consequences because this was a serious game we were playing. Like I said I was bound by my Laws, so I kept it in the hood, but Blanks did business with all sorts of people not just Mexican but white bikers, stoners, strippers, and construction workers. But he wasn't an independent. He knew who to ask and when to ask before he made moves.

Just because he had an arsenal at his disposal didn't mean he walked around thinking he was 'Lucky Luciano'. He had much respect for Gang Law and carried himself with dignity & honor. I respected him and maybe that's why I took the same to him as Bugs had done for me so many years ago when it came to the age thing.

My life on the home front was in pretty good shape. Moms was happy I wasn't doing drugs anymore although I was around them all day long. I had overcome any and all temptations to do drugs, and like this great cholo once said "I don't do drugs, I don't even like drugs but they're there". Of course, I still had the state people on me for my past aggressions. They checked me at home once a month and had me pee in a bottle twice a month.

Remember in the beginning of this story I said the King of the neighborhood was this big cat called 'T' which he still was but like I said times were changing and the violence had escalated to more gunfire than fists. He was old school and really didn't need a gun; he was more into beating the living crap out of someone if they got out of line.

Anyway, he knew what I was doing in the neighborhood and for my part I was doing everything according to Gang Law except one thing I overlooked and that was a big one. I never talked to him about what I was doing. Needless to say, he wasn't at all pleased about that. So, before I knew it the rumors and shit talking was spreading around the neighborhood. So, when the opportunity arose, I dealt with it. I confronted him in the back yard and for a guy of 300 plus pounds this mother moved fast.

We started throwing blows in the back yard and worked our way to the side of the house as one of my partners and one of his was trying to break us up. In the end he hit the ground first and soon after it was over. I explain this fight to you in this manner because back then and maybe even today if one raised a hand against me unless he was a good homie, he became my enemy for life. But this man was king of my neighborhood and felt disrespected that I would try this bold move without asking for his blessing or even if he wanted in.

But by my way of thinking I had been taken advantage of by his peers and fought them to establish myself. So, I just went ahead with my plans and felt I would deal with anybody that got in my way. So, when he and I locked horns, I felt he was satisfied with what had transpired between us and now he would let me have the throne. I truly believe that this was all he wanted from me, was the recognition a man of his stature deserved.

My bad. I did say I was blinded by ambition and greed and all those other sick details that make a man do stupid shit. He continued roaming around the hood only now I was in the driver's seat and he was happy. Maybe even relived that he no longer had to defend everybody that came to him with a problem. Oh yes, it was now my turn to take care of the neighborhood.

Aside from being in the business I was in, I now made sure that our fallen homeboys did not die in vain. I enforced the rules "T" had set. I made sure his legacy would be honored but mostly I implemented the game plan Tony had outlined for us! With Blanks' business acumen and my street battle smarts, we became a force to be reckoned with. And so it went that Blanks brought in some of his people and I supplied the troops and off and running we went. Clocking dollars and building our little empire.

CHAPTER

I know it sounds like with Tony & Blanks, I was always number 2 during these times, it's not that at all. I was a military genius and the guys I ran with couldn't pull off the muscle I could. Even when Blanks went away for a couple of years, I still ran the show like it should have been run. I was also still very heavily involved with my gang shenanigans. I say shenanigans because it's been many, many years since those days.

Looking back, I wonder just how the fuck I survived. I say with pride that not one of my homeboys will ever tell you I ran from a fight and all of them will tell you I was always in the front of the battle. So along with doing business, making money, and having a blast, I was also running the streets of my neighborhood, protecting, serving, and smashing those that got out of line.

The people that lived there were comfortable with me running the streets and doing what had to be done to keep the riffraff out of their back yards. Writing on walls by the youngsters was regulated. I even had some come back and paint over their artwork because it was the wrong house or wall to write on. I remember once I was making my rounds and decided to take a short cut through some yards and as I was about to jump a fence in between the house and some apartments, this girl asks through her window "Nano, is that you?" I simply said "Yeah" and kept on my way.

Another time, and this is a fond memory for me, I was walking down 42nd street. Dressed like the gang member I was. Bandana under my ball cap, t-shirt and 501's, and of course my beloved "Chucks" or Converse if you don't know what Chucks are. When this little old lady stops me and calls me into her yard.

I have no idea who she is or what she wants. I walk up to her and with respect I say "Buenas tardes" and she hands me a light bulb and says to me in Spanish "Change this light bulb" pointing to her porch light fixture. It was a small house but still I couldn't reach the other light to change it, so I look around and found a small table.

I slid this small table under the light and begin to climb up but then my gun gets in the way, so I step back down and pull my gun out and hand it to her and tell her in Spanish "Here, hold this" and she stands there holding my gun in her little old hands as I changed her porch light. When I was done, I climbed down, and she handed me my gun back and said "Gracias" and I said, "De nada" and continued on my way.

I prevented a war or two in those days. As much as I liked violence, I wasn't crazy about going to funerals. I attended many of them back in the day. Friends and foes fell in those days. Some deserved it, some were just caught in the wrong place at the wrong time. It was a vicious time then. Then there were the drug users. Many, many guys I grew up with fell into a drug stupor that few ever recover from. Some were lucky because drugs will eat you up, and when it's done eating you physically it will eat your mind and then your soul.

There are many different opinions on this subject but for those that never lived in the barrios or had to fight your way home from school because you lived in a different neighborhood than where the school is located, your opinion doesn't matter. All I'm saying is that I speak from the heart and experience on this particular issue. I started doing drugs at an early age and hit it as hard as I could. It is said that the men of my family abuse the pleasures of life which went on for a good portion of my life. The drug scene was bad for many of us.

To feel bad about it now makes me feel hypocritical because for a good portion of my life selling these drugs is what I did for a living. But I don't think that this is the point I am trying to make here. I want to talk about the boys that never made it to manhood, the good women that became whores behind this. Drugs have a way of taking your will power away, no matter how strong you may think you are. Many guys who were trusted in this game we played became un-trustworthy.

Johnny was a good dude, a shy fella who had heart for days, was built like an Aztec Warrior, wasn't the most handsome guy around but solid as a rock. We went through early teens together riding bikes on Sammy's Trails then graduating to stealing cars. The transition was easy because we had stolen bikes together so stealing cars came easy. But then one day somewhere, someone did the unthinkable. Not only did Johnny break his oath to never fuck with this, but he also accepted someone's offer to slam some dope.

It went downhill from there he even had a cool job, worked in a clothing store, and got sweet discounts on dress clothes. First the job goes, then the car, next thing you know he gets kicked out of his house. He began doing scandalous shit, at first it was just little shit, but soon would get bigger and it started affecting his relationship with the fellas. He then started burning his homeboys. Then one day he died, hit by a car running across the freeway. He met with such a gruesome death! I know what I'm saying is a story echoed throughout the years of how a good dude goes bad and becomes just another soul lost to the dark side. Soul after soul went to the dark side, those that did come back were far and few in between

I was fortunate enough to come back with my mind still intact, everything was beat the hell up, my body at its worst weighed 120 pounds. Not good at all for a man 27 years of age, financially I was ruined; my kids were strangers to me. Most of my family had written me off. I had seen death, destruction all around me.

A good friend of mine had just got out of prison after about 6 years and came to my house one night. He decided to visit me and saw me at my worst. I truly believe it broke his heart to see his friend & best homie tore up from the floor up. I noticed the look in his eyes and said to him "I look like I'm to the curb, don't I?" He just nodded with a sad look on his face. Looking him in the eye, I said "I may have lost my mind, but I haven't lost my heart, no one is stepping on my toes".

Hoping that would satisfy him but he was coming from Folsom State Prison where a sign of weakness can get one killed. So, whether he believed me or not, we went on about our business. In short time he was back in the big house for another nickels worth of years. I on the other hand turned my shit around and re-entered this game that I started so long ago. After that short prison term, I regrouped and ventured into this next level of gangsterism with the skills I learned as a child and honed throughout the years. I kept my circle small. To this day my name is known but more than half of them don't even know what I looked like back then.

I hooked up with Blanks & company. We had to work out the kinks as in any business. We fell into a good system of selling drugs all the while he ran his crew of midnight thieves, and I ran my neighborhood according to Gang Law. We always managed to find time to go eat somewhere. We never really had a favorite spot although we did have a favorite food. Living in southern California it's the biggest game in town!

Mexican Food, man there were a million and one taco shops starting with Roberto's to Hilberto's, Gilberto's, Adalberto's, and the list went on. Add to that the fine Mexican Food dining establishments. Ah man we ate good! One time we were on a mission or headed to one and I said I was hungry, and Blanks said "Business first" so I agreed but all of a sudden without saying a word, Blanks spins this monster truck we driving in around and starts heading in the opposite direction? I ask, "what's up?" Blanks says in the coolest way "fuck that, as long as we got money, we'll never be hungry" who was I to argue with that logic.

The beginning of our enterprise consisted of us figuring out who would we recruit to sell our product, I already had my regular customers in the neighborhood, and I know Blanks had his around this fine city. Our issue was that as we grew, our supplies would get larger and we would eventually need a new safe spot to keep, count, weigh and clean our stuff, basically we'd need an office (of sorts). One day as we were cruising around taking care of business, we passed by this warehouse looking building, it consisted of a small house set to the side by the main gate, with a very large driveway and a large garage/workshop out back.

As we drove by, I recognized this small ugly ass green truck parked in the driveway, "Hold up, backup" I said. "I'd recognize that ugly ass truck anywhere". It belonged to a customer of mine who used to come over to Squirrels house to buy dope while I was house-sitting for Squirrel. Anyways Squirrel owed me some money and I couldn't find his ass anywhere in the neighborhood because of this little thing we had going on, and once I saw this truck, I figured he might know. So, Blanks backs up and stops in front of this driveway. I jump out and walk cautiously up to the workshop.

Dude pops up from below a car, all he heard was someone walking into his business so thinking it was a customer he pops up with smile on his face and forming words of welcome but when he sees me his smile gets even bigger and hey says "hey man, what's up, what are you doing around here?" then after a few pleasantries, I ask "have you seen Squirrel?" To which he responds with a little apprehension in his voice as he's most certainly heard about the little incident I had with Squirrel. He says that he hasn't seen or heard from Squirrel in a while.

Jimmy gives me the tour of his business; I knew he was a welder by trade, but I never knew he had his own business let alone where he lived. Of course, he told me he lived over by so and so but to be honest I didn't really care. He was a customer he might have been cool, but our friendship didn't go beyond that of him coming over to Squirrels house, getting his little bag of dope and making small talk. But now seeing his place and seeing that it was well away from our current base of operations.

A plan started taking shape in these collective criminal minded heads of ours, soon after we struck a deal. He would let us use his office for our business and we would pay his rent. We also kept a safe there to protect our goodies from anybody that might want to take "just a little bit" This arrangement went pretty well for quite some time even after Blanks went away.

We were able to keep large amounts on hand for the bigger clients that weren't used to waiting. Don't get me wrong we treated all of our clients with respect. Good service is what got us over the top and put money in our pockets. "Within the hour" Blanks would say. I was at a wedding once way out at one of the Indian casinos and needless to say it was a banging wedding, old family I hadn't seen for a spell, I was having an awesome time. When I get a call "Go see Daisy and John" which meant they needed their usual, $3,600 for an hour's worth of work.

Ok so I'm about an hour out from our office, which will most definitely be locked up, so I have to open the big gate, kill the alarm, make the package and then 20 minutes out to Daisy's and after to Jon's. I was back at the casino in 2 hours with 2 happy customers. Yes, I missed a few dances and maybe an argument between two drunk uncles but hey the night was still young. To this day I still can't figure out why my cousin would want to hold a reception so far away. But it was an awesome wedding, nonetheless. Everyone was happy, clients, guests, and the boss. As in all businesses the bottom line is the dollar.

About a year into our merger, Blanks went away for a couple years. Man, that really messed a lot of people up. This kid had an extraordinary way of conducting himself and the businesses he ran. He had a loyal following from his crew, his family ties were unique to say the least. We lost many contacts from down south, many dealers we had on the payroll jumped ship because they would rather deal with somebody else than with my vicious ass. I wasn't past socking someone that didn't have all the money on hand when we came for it. This put us in a tailspin for a minute, but I had been through worse, so I got my guys and we regrouped until Blanks would be returned to us. I gotta tell you though that in that first year, we made a ton of money, made a ton of enemies, and had more fun than criminals should be allowed too.

So, it was settled, he would later receive a proper homecoming when the time was right. But right now, I had a neighborhood to look out for and money to make. I secured the open sides of our business and tied up that which needed to be tied up for now, Blanks would deal with them when he came back. Yes, profits were slashed way down due to my commitments and boundaries. I was relegated to my side of town. I didn't cross Barrio borders to deal drugs. I kept it short but sweet. I would not have to answer to bigger fish, I answered to those I answered to.

Pretty soon I had my area sewed up. There were a couple free spirits doing their thing but not enough to bother me, except one old fool that wanted to run his mouth and said no one can tax him or some stupid shit, so I head hunted him down and when I found him, he was at a buddies house near the border of the neighborhood to our south, maybe this fool thought nobody would find him there. I showed up and had his narrow ass brought out to me. After making him empty his pockets I let him know if he ever runs his mouth again like that, I would have all the furniture from his house removed and sold.

I was mean, strict and hella vicious, but it was also known I was a man of my word and just. I never let power, money or fame go to my head. It just wasn't taught to me by those I looked up to, admired and respected, I took care of family, friends, and homies, and not necessarily in that order either. Business in the Barrio was good for a couple of years. Things were pretty smooth, yes there were some boneheads doing bonehead things, but they would usually straighten themselves out before I got a hold of them.

Eventually Blanks got out and came back with a vengeance, he held no grudges against the shit talkers, and believe me there were a couple of them running their mouths behind some false rumors that had started but nothing to get in a tizzy over. Nor did he see any problem with picking up right where he left off. Or as he would often say "Now where was I before I was so rudely interrupted?"

This man came back with a plan and nothing and nobody was going to stop him. One of his first victims were these out of towners that had decided to set up shop in our neighborhood without consulting anyone from the neighborhood, how this fool got by my detection is beyond me, but it sometimes seemed Blanks had more eyes and ears than I had.

I remember we caught this fool walking across the street. Thinking his shit don't stink and as I approached him, he stopped dead in his tracks and as I was calmly letting him know that this was our neighborhood and wasn't gonna sell dope here without paying rent. I removed the gold chain he was wearing and put it in my pocket to show him I was not playing. He nodded and said "I understand" then arrangements were made for him to pay once a week. Things went smooth for about a month until he got stupid and tried to shoot it out with the fellas over the week's payment.

Blanks was ready to take this shit to a different level, I didn't know there were more levels to this shit, but I guess I was wrong. So, what the hell, let's do this. He went straight to his old contacts and got the ball rolling. He brought in some new people on his side which is cool. He would call me to his place on top of the hill and we'd unload and get situated for the next day's business, all the while going over the books of our little empire in the making.

Yes, sir things were going good if this is the lifestyle you choose to be in. We had the office at Jimmy's, our bank accounts were getting fat. Of course, you understand that by that I mean our safes were getting full. We dealt in a cash business so it wasn't like we could just go to any bank and deposit such large amounts of money. But again, Blanks was playing on a different level now. In his studies while he was away, he learned the real estate game among other legal games that would help us invest our earnings instead of blowing $10,000 on a ring "because you think you're in love!" We invested in properties out of state for a while, a house here, a house there, a small taco shop there. Had us a summer and winter house, even though we lived in sunshine all year around, we still found time to go out of town for a few days here and there. New Year's Eve in Vegas was always cool. We'd stayed at a friend's house and enjoyed the New Year's celebration on the strip very V.I.P style too. We would be escorted into casinos the same way rock stars were and we'd exit them like rock stars too.

CHAPTER

It was during these fun times that my mother began to get sick and fall a lot. It really bummed me out to see her with all these tubes up her nose and IV's in her arm. It was hard for me as she was my world. During the dark years of my life, she was the only one in my family that never turned her back on me. Even when my siblings would tell her "Call the cops and have him thrown out of here" or whatever it was they would say to her. She would just say "es mi hijo" which means "he's my son!" So, I guess in hindsight I see what she meant now when she would tell me the same thing about my brothers, not that I would call the cops on my brothers, but it would really roast my weenie seeing my brothers take advantage of my mother's kindness.

It was not an easy pill to swallow, don't get me wrong, I gave them hell over it. But she was moms and what moms said was law at home. She had many ailments but man that lady was tough, beautiful soul and tough from the old country, and man could she cook, even when we was poor, she would hook up some cabbage and sausage for us, I really miss her cooking these days. Therefore, whenever she was in the hospital, no matter where I was or what I was doing I always made the time to go see her and talk to her or feed her dinner. The nurses all would give me odd looks because here I was looking straight like a gangster with bodyguards, and I would be feeding this little old lady her dinner.

She was my mother, one time after everyone had gone home or at least out of the room she asked me what was wrong? I told her in Spanish that no one understood me, and she patted my head and said "me voy a mejorar, mijo me nesesita" this type of events would go on for years.

At one point I was at one hospital visiting one of my homeboys' mom because he was doing "Life" up state, and there was another fella there visiting also. After saying our goodbyes to her we both walked out together and in the parking lot. We shake hands and were about to part ways when I say, "Thanks for coming OG" he asks me where I'm headed to, and I respond "I'm gonna go see my mom now". Which must have blown his mind because he we are visiting one woman and now, I was about to go visit another. He was genuinely surprised that I would be doing something like that. Then he said, "Man I feel bad for you" I told him "Don't feel bad for me ese, I'm here visiting their mom because they can't be here". (Her other son had been murdered years earlier).

Life was teaching me things I knew were there but had vaguely paid attention too in the past. I was seeing things in a different light; most things in general seemed to take a different shine in my eyes. Don't get me wrong, my loyalty was to my neighborhood and those around me, yes, my mom was my world, but without my career I was pretty much just a lump of meat.

The meaning of life was changing for me, not noticeably but little by little I started seeing life from the other side of the spectrum and this spectrum is in no way like the normal life spectrum. My life was anything but normal. I remember this friend of mine was at my house waiting for me to get there, and when I do, I'm rather tired since I would go a day or 2 sometimes without sleep and as I sit back oh so comfortably on my lounger chair, they commented on my attire and said, "Normal niggas don't wear pinstripes and leather jackets" I said "I'm not a normal nigga". For the most part it was OK, I guess. But I might be getting ahead of myself again. Life in the Barrio was changing, new blood was coming in. My star wasn't as shinny as it used to be, don't get me wrong, my name alone still struck fear in those that would oppose me, but it was me myself that was feeling different about all this.

I was surrounded by people every day, yet I was feeling very much alone, a cliché maybe? Maybe not, I don't know because, I never really cared about anything else other than my world in the Barrio. Blanks was always busy setting up deals all over the place. I could have sworn the man never slept, but of course he did it just seemed like he never did. The man was on his toes, which is to say his internal wheels were well greased and turning at all times.

I could literally see the wheels in his head turning one time when I told him that the low-rider parked down the street was locked but had the keys in the ignition. You're talking about at least 5 thousand dollars' worth of equipment in it along with chrome rims & a sick ass stereo system. It truly was a sight to see him jump into action and to see how he would organize his crew with their perspective jobs. Everyone was well trained in what they needed to do. One would get a getaway car; another would open the garage. He even had one guy just go to a 7/11 and get potato chips and soda. Yes, sir this man was definitely on his toes.

And as for me, well I was busy running the neighborhood, my stores were running good. I had one store in particular that was being run by a woman (not by choice). But she seemed to know her business. I never liked women in this business I'm old fashioned. Early in them days women were picking up game and getting involved in on it. I mean they've always been there on the side. But some were taking advantage of the situations around them and becoming dealers themselves. Gina was her name; she had her own store for a while until I dropped in on her one night. I was in need of a little something and one of my guys says in Spanish, "Let's go over to this dame's house I know". Very soon after that visit, she was selling my product and so I ended up allowing her to stay open.

Only problem was she had this brother that would like to hang out there. I never really met him but one night he was there and had quite a buzz going when we showed up for the nightly take. He was surprised at how we entered the house, first one guy would go in and clear the house of any unwanted people, then my bodyguard would enter, then I would enter followed by a couple other boys.

We would post up and chill for a while and made sure things were cool, it was about that time that I would step into Gina's office, and she would lay out the money for me on the desk. I never took money from someone's hand. Anyways when I stepped in her office, I noticed some dude sitting at her desk. I'm thinking "who the hell is this?" there wasn't supposed to be anyone in there (You best believe I was gonna dig in my boy's ass for not clearing the room). But turns out dude was her brother, so I didn't mind it too much. But before I picked up anything from the desk, I noticed all the testosterone floating around the room.

Dude was sizing me up and I'm sure I know what he was thinking "I can take him" a lot of people seem to think that because I was still short. I didn't grow much throughout my life so at 5'6" people always thought I was an easy take, especially the drunk ones. Boy was they in for a shocking surprise. My bodyguard once told me it was hard to be my bodyguard because I was always pushing him out the way to get at some fool or other. Dude says to me with this serious look on his face "Sup" so I say "Sup" back. His sister introduces us, but he didn't extend his hand and neither did I. Instead, I told homegirl "I'll be in the living room" and without picking up the money I walked out.

A few minutes later she walked out to the living room, then her brother followed but he stopped short in the doorway. He looks around at my guys and says, "There's a lot of mother fuckers in here tonight" then he adds "Mother fuckers I don't know" and at this point he lunges at my boy Oscar, grabbing him by the throat yelling "Like you" and in what reminded me of the Secret Service, my guys had this guy pinned to the wall and floor within seconds.

My bodyguard had pushed me into a hallway and blocked my body with his, facing me, we had a way of communicating with just our eyes so when he stared at me, I knew what he wanted so I complied. My boys roughed him up a little bit just to get him to calm the fuck down. He kept talking stupid like most drunk people do, repeating himself and what not, trying to get his point across. So, I look at my bodyguard and he smiles and steps aside and I walk over to where the guy is standing. He's surrounded by my guys, I say to him very calmly "We didn't come here to disrespect you, your sister or this house but I'm gonna tell you something, we ain't no punks and we ain't no mother fuckers". So, he straightens up and says "You're showing me respect but this punk mother fucker..." I cut him off and repeated myself "Like I said dude we ain't no punks and we ain't no mother fuckers" he stomps his feet and throws his fists up in the air and yells "I don't give a fuck who you..." I hit this fool in the mouth about 4 or 5 times before he bounced off the wall and my guys were beating the crap out of him. As I Backed up and let them have at it with his face. By this time Oscar had jumped into action and had gone to get the cars backing them up in the driveway for a getaway. My guys cleared a path for me as I walked outside and waited for all my guys to come out. We had other stops before the night would be over. For about a month after I would just send somebody to collect. I eventually stopped by and guess who was there? Yes, sir her brother. Funny thing though is dude didn't even recognize me and he still had the markings of a black eye.

These and other events were taking place all around the neighborhood. But it is what it is. If you chose this life, you are either in all the way or you become a victim of it. And I saw a lot of people become victims. I did what I had to do but my life was changing. At one point one of my guys decided to go into business for him-self so he set up shop around the corner and proceeded to do his thing, but again those independents can fly under the radar for only so long before it gets to the wrong ears.

He happened to set up shop next door to where some of the neighborhood thugs would kick back and soon enough, they started noticing an unusual amount of traffic going to this house and upon investigation they realized this cat was doing business on their turf (there are rules about this). It was quite well known that once you set up shop in a known neighborhood, you must first speak with the right people and make sure no toes are being stepped on.

If dues are owed, then that too will be arranged. It is when these individuals decide to circumvent these rules that things don't end well as you are well aware from Blanks first move upon his release. So, this one particular incident was a touchy one because the guy was part of my crew and the fellas were well aware of this, so at first, they didn't bother him thinking it was one of my stores, and since a couple of them knew this guy personally they would drop by for a little kick down.

Then one day dude decided he didn't want to kick the fellas down with a little get high for the night. The issue of paying rent was brought up first amongst them 2 then amongst the fellas. Eventually it came across my desk. It wasn't long after that that one of the fellas came to me with the question. Was this guy under my wing (protection, partner, associate, etc.) he asked.

Turns out he was but for other reasons. He wasn't running one of my stores, which was a key point here. But as he was part of my crew, so this dude was well aware of the rules. Then right after that visit I was paid another visit by my boy. He came to me for many reasons but one especially, his lady was from the neighborhood and although technically not from the hood he was a very good associate of. So, he comes to me after his lady had advised him that before things get heavy or ugly or both, he needed to come see me.

He drops by one afternoon and the discussion went pretty well. It was these conversations that were really becoming irrelevant to me, like I didn't care anymore. It was a really confusing time for me, but I was who I was so deal with these issues I did. I gotta say that I've been in the game long enough to know how people think when it comes to people in my position in this game. Back then I was very in tune with people's gestures, people's motives to why they would say what they said to me.

I was a master of bullshitting people. I once even talked myself out handcuffs, with the heat saying, "We'll be in touch" yeah whatever mother fucker. So, the conversation with my boy goes like this: "Hey brother can I talk to you?" he asks. "What's up youngster?" I answered he then lets me know that he has been doing a little some, some with his lady (I figured he mentioned her for safety reasons). He said to help make ends meet blah, blah, blah, now I already know what's going on over there because of my conversations earlier with one of the fellas. So, I sit there and listen to his story nodding in agreement as I know what it is to struggle every once in a while, but and this is a serious, 'But' this man has been doing business on my territory! First of all, he is doing so without permission, 2nd not paying rent. Let alone that it isn't my merchandise he is selling! I'm already angered by that one. Pissed off to no end as a matter of fact, but like I said this is a special case as this guy is one of my own.

He then asks, "do I need to pay rent?" So, after he finishes saying what he needed to say. I walk towards the door and turn around facing him. I do my best to hide my anger; this is business I tell myself. To him I growl "This is Business!" Adding "You went behind my back and set up shop. On my turf and it's not even my shit!" What the hell could possibly go wrong in this situation dude has created for himself?

He has this look of confusion on his face. Did he think all would be hunky dory? Did he think there would be no consequences? What the hell was this idiot thinking? I'm only referring to him as an idiot because I was angry, he was far from an idiot, or he would never have been part of my crew. I was a serious man a man not to be trifled with. I was very clear with everybody in what was expected of my people. The roles everyone played had to be played for keeps. There were no blood oaths like the Italian Mafia you understand but still this was a serious game we were involved in, and I expected serious people. I told him "Yes" in Spanish "You do have to pay rent!" But it would not be to me he would have to pay.

Because of his actions of setting up shop on my turf and getting chesty with the fellas, I came to this conclusion. He asked, "Then to who?" I said, "The fellas" and he thought about it for a minute and said "OK, but how much?" Not exactly sure why he would think about it because there was no way around this outcome, and I responded "If you make $100 dollars, give them 20" I added "And if you make 20 then give them 5" to which he readily agreed. Then just to drive the severity of this situation, I drop it on him, "But don't play them ese, don't make 100 and tell them all you made is 20" I assured him that I would make sure only one guy would go see him at the end of each day to collect. He was now part of my system; he no longer was in the inner circle of my crew.

He now belonged on the client's side of the equation. For that he would get their protection and his house would be safe. He asks me "What will they do with the money?" Surprised by this odd question, I tell him "Whatever the fuck they want to this is their hood, ese" So the terms were set, and he was given the green light to carry on.

Remember I did say what could go wrong didn't I? Well, this fool started off doing ok. One fella would go at the end of each day to collect and for the most part everyone was cool with it. But money has a way of fucking up one's way of thinking about shit. One gets greedy or goes into debt by spending more than he's making. Or even worse one starts to think he's untouchable. Most likely this knucklehead did all of them.

But the one that almost cost him his life was he played them. Of course, I was kept abreast of everything going on over there. I had to be if I was gonna keep my neighborhood safe. I needed to know who was up to no good so they could be dealt with accordingly. I'm telling you it was hard being the neighborhood drug dealer and night watchman. But serve my neighborhood I did. I would have people patrolling the area for undesirables.

Even though I never got into the heroin scene; it was all around, and dope fiends don't care about nothing but getting high. They would do it in a car, in the alley, behind the school. They would slam their shit and throw dirty needles anywhere. They started doing it in my alley and one day I walked up on them and pointed my double barrel shotgun at them, and very calmly I let them know that if one of my kids caught aids behind their stupidity, they would all die. They stopped littering.

By now my guy was making good money, and I never hated on him for that, jealousy was never in my blood. This is why I was not charging him rent; I let the fellas do their thing. I also told the little homie "Watch him and don't let him play you" But sure enough my boy got stupid. One night the assigned fella goes to see him, and dude says, "I haven't' sold anything today" so the little homie leaves but the 2nd night when he goes and dude says he didn't have anything because he hadn't sold anything, the little homie pulls a little pipe out and says, "Well then just hook me up with a little some, some for the night." My boy says "No!" Bad choice of words for him to utter. You see the fellas on my advice watched his house and every person walking out was stopped and asked how much they scored? "I just got a 40" or "I just scored a teener" of course these people were gonna answer these questions. The fellas were fucking hardcore gang members, the people were just happy the fellas weren't taking their shit.

This stuff adds up in a 12-hour day. So, when my boy refuses to give the homie a little some, some the homie cracks him upside the head and takes his stash, then tells him "And I'll be back again tomorrow".

As in all places of ill refute people like to gather and chill. So, by now my boy had accumulated some guys of his own, older fellas from the hood, still around but too old to put in work. When they showed up and saw their guy with a lump on his head and no dope to share, they decided to take matters into their own hands.

They asked, "Who did this?" What they should have asked is "why" but by this time in their lives they felt entitled for living this type of life and still being alive. So, I take it they were upset that there was no dope for them. That and the story dude gave them put them on the defense for him.

Anyhow these fools piled into one fools' car and took a little trip down to the homies house and did what is called a 'Bum-rush' and ran into the house without knocking and totally disrespecting the house. There are rules about this but when a fool feels like the rules don't apply to him for whatever reason they tend to do the stupidest of things. Before I continue, I have to let you know that although it was 4 dudes that went to this house, only 3 entered because as I head hunted these hombres down one at a time, the first being the older homie from the hood.

Then within a weeks' time I caught one at the car wash or better, yet he caught up to me at the car wash and told me that he was there but never entered the house because when they arrived, he saw whose house it was and knew there was going to be consequences. He knew that house was under my protection, and he had been around long enough to know that these were not the kind of consequences he wanted to have to deal with. I believed him because his name was never mentioned as to who entered the house that day so with my blessings he went on his way.

They ran into the house and attacked the homie and tried throwing him out the 2nd story Window. They managed to stab him in the head a couple of times. Then when one of my younger homegirls came out of her room and tells these fools to get out of her house. The older homie turns around and backhands her across the face, sending her flying across the room. I'm just glad her mom wasn't there at the time all this went down. I had a special respect for this lady. This lady came from an old neighborhood family, a family that had seen much tragedy. Both drugs and gang violence had plagued this family throughout the years I believe there were like 6 brothers, and more than half died violently or over dosed, either way this family had seen a lot of shit. Left to raise her kids alone when her husband died (he was one of the brothers) she did her best. She worked the minimal jobs afforded a low educated widow from the hood with 4 kids. Yes, they turned out to be semi hoodlums but good people, nonetheless.

So, when this knucklehead wanna be gangster hit my little homegirl, she got up and ran to my house. Or walked very fast because I was a few blocks up the way. When she got there, she told me what had gone down at her house. When she told me who it was, I knew where to find them. We jumped into my car and took a little ride over to my boys' house. I told her to wait in the car. She had a nice view as I was parked in the driveway.

As I walked up to the front door, I saw that the front door was open but had a wrought iron door. I knocked and my older homie whom I respected since I met him when I was just a wee lad, came to the door acting just like a guy that had just did some dirt. No shirt on, flashing tattoos with his dark gang member glasses. He says "What's up little homie" it wasn't a question, it was more a greeting. I said "Come outside ese I want to talk to you" to which he responded that the door was locked and if I wanted to talk, I should come around through the back.

So, I stepped back and said again "Come outside ese, I want to talk to you" my voice wasn't cheerful at all. I too was in full gang uniform with t-shirt, bandana & Levi's along with my chucks. He says "Alright" knowing full well we were going to chunk some blows the minute he stepped outside. As I'm waiting for him to come around the girl who actually lived in the house came to the door and was surprised that it was me standing there knocking on her door, she greeted me and after I told her I was waiting for dude. She said nonsense, that this was her house, and I would come in through the front door, a sign of respect. As she was unlocking the wrought iron door the older fella came walking around the corner from the side of the house. Remember I said I respected Gang Law and one of them is to respect your older homeboys.

Which I do to this day but after all the bullshit that Bugs had taught us to beware of. I wasn't above smashing a fool in the mouth if he deserved it, older homie or not.

So here I am, and it wasn't the first time I busted up an older homie over some neighborhood business. He was a sight though, he had our gang logo tattooed across his chest, so it brought emotion to the forefront, but I was pretty upset with this fool, so emotions be damned. I walked up to him and said, "Why you put hands on the homegirl ese?" he said, "I didn't do anything ese" I said, "How about I put hands on you?" as he was pulling off his shades he said "You gotta do what you gotta do" and that was exactly what I did. I hit him with a right on his left cheek; he backed up a bit and threw what is known as a hammer.

That's when a person puts all his weight behind one punch in order to knock out his opponent. Needless to say, he missed; I then proceeded to do what I like to call a 'De La Hoya' on his crusty, disrespecting ass. Meaning I lit his ass up! Punch after punch I landed on his face and try as I might I gotta give it to this old dude, he never went down. I'm sure he had a vicious headache afterwards. He would throw a hammer every now and then, but none made contact, I promise you.

By now everyone in the house had come out running. One homegirl was saying to me "I did it, I hit her" by then I just stopped hitting dude. My boy was there looking all kinds of nervous (oh he knew). So, I stepped back and with my arm extended I pointed to all of them and said, "I'm here because of what he did, he got what he got for putting hands on a homegirl!" I said to my boy while poking my finger into chest "You will answer for what you did, not to me but to the homeboys!" Needless to say, he went on the lam after that little episode. I found out later that he did a little state time, got out and learned a trade and then hooked up with some dame he met somewhere along his road to normalcy and went on to live a normal life.

Can't say that I blame dude for it, our world was a crazy ass world. Far apart from the rest of the world, I guess you could say that a lot of these events that occurred from time to time in my neighborhood would end up having everlasting effects of people. Like I said new blood was coming into the Barrio, things were and will always change with time. It is inevitable that these things happen. It was happening for me during these times. I still had to act accordingly but things were changing.

I remember I had a dispute with one fool that as we sat there, he was on the couch, I was in a lounge chair pointing guns at one another and I asked him if he was willing to die over this. Because I was, he then slowly raised his hands in a peace or surrender gesture. Says he is going outside to smoke a cigarette "So please don't shoot." I Haven't seen that fool ever since, he left everything he owned behind (wasn't much) we had been roommates sharing a studio and when he left, dude just disappeared into the night and next thing I know he turned his life around and got as far away from this madness as he could.

I understand now that these are considered near death experiences and will affect some in ways that cannot be explained. Maybe they can but psychology is not taught at the 'The School of Hard Knocks' which is in fact where one of my degrees is from. What could be going through your head when for the past year you are dealing in stolen goods, and I'm talking an 18-wheeler full of shit, electrical tools, air tools, TV's and we even had a nice electrical train once, not sure where that came from, but it sold for half the going store price. Think you are just the coolest mother fucker to walk the earth. Carry a gun in a shoulder holster, and then someone points a gun at you and asks if you are willing to die for it? And your first choice is to run away and walk the path of the righteous?

This is what I mean. If you gonna play, play for keeps. I did, I played for keeps, and I knew the consequences of what could happen while I was doing the shit I was doing. I also knew there could, and would be jail if I was caught, I knew that death was right there ready to pounce on me at any moment. This was a serious game I had chosen to play from a very young age. Why I chose to play this game is a question for the ages, I just know that I did, and something inside me drove me to the limits of what one could do. I tempted faith like no other; I dodged many a bullet in those days. People wondered why I grew so much gray hair.

CHAPTER

With Blanks it was always a little less violent but always intriguing, for instance he was having issues with this one kid but didn't know where he lived. So, One day Blanks has someone put a tracking device on his car and as I wasn't too much into technology back then, I was incredibly impressed when we opened the app and saw the way this kid drove home. Simple as that, we had a location. We scoped out the layout a few times before we moved in and hit this guy's stash while he was out on a date. Boring yes because I would rather just confront this numbnut in the street and whoop his ass, but Blanks was more sophisticated than that.

He liked to hit them in their pockets or if you really pissed him off, he'd send in the 'Stud'. The Stud was this guy with an exotic background, tall, good-looking, well-built hunk. He could sweet-talk a girl out of her panties with ease. He would go after the opponents' girl and let's just say he would get them in very compromising positions (with pictures) and somehow these pictures would find their way to said opponent's mailbox.

Blanks was a cold-hearted man when it came to business and would utilize any and all weapons at his disposal and unfortunately for his opponents, he was crafty as hell and ruthlessly smart. I sometimes wondered if he even had a soul. Don't get me wrong, this guy was not evil. He never intentionally hurt someone or bankrupted them. He carried himself in an honorable way. I'm just saying that once someone thought they could outsmart him or burn him during a business deal, it was then that the dark side of his essence would come out. Even the guys from his crew were like this. They never started anything, but man once someone went there against them, all the stops were pulled out and revenge would be served in heaps.

One time the Stud was at a party over by his neighborhood, and this kid thought he could bully the Stud because he had some of his "bros" there and the stud was by himself. They decided to surround him on the dance floor and start with the tough talk. I remember I was home in my driveway working on my low-rider, when Blanks pulls up and says, "Get in" so as I start to close the hood of my car he shouts, "No time!" I knew then that this was serious, so I just jumped the fence and hopped in his van.

Off we go headed towards the freeway, as I asked, "Where we going?" A smooth ass AK-47 came sliding over my shoulder into my lap. To which I just say "Fuck it, let's ride" we headed south on the freeway and worked our way to the house where the Stud was at. Took us all of 10 minutes to get there driving 95 MPH. He was waiting for us out on the sidewalk when we got there. He jumps in and after I finished teasing him about letting some punks' disrespect him, he told Blanks they were going to some person's house. I didn't know these fools, but Blanks and the Stud went to school together they knew the same people. So, Blanks knew exactly where to go, we pull up in a cul-de-sac behind a small car with rims of the day, 2 or 3 guys were sitting in it laughing and seemed a bit proud of themselves for having bullied a rather popular guy.

I swear sometimes I wonder how these idiots ever made it past high school playing on the same field we played on. We pulled up right behind them with our lights off and they didn't even hear us. We got out of the van walked up on both sides of their car, and the only thing they heard was the sound of 6 guns being cocked. The laughter died instantly, as we made them exit the car, hands up, and the Stud lays into the main guy and beats him like a red headed stepchild. Then after explaining to these idiots, to be sure who you get in the ring with next time.

As quietly as we pulled up is as quietly as we drove off, my point here being that we didn't need 6 guns to just kick one dudes ass. But as Blanks and his guys would like to say, "Pump the fear of God into them" which is what I mean when I say that they would pull out all the stops to make their point about anything. Not always violent; that was just my example of the extremeness they would go to scare them fuckers straight.

Blanks was always the cool, calm guy, always joking around. Never one to be stingy with his money or turn his back on someone from the hood in need of help, always opened his house to anyone in need of some food or shower. But cross him once though, and he was like the Italians and held a grudge forever. I'm serious, there are people walking around 20 years down the road still wondering why they ever decided to do this young man wrong.

What really amazed me was his abstinence from drugs. He had been dealing in them for years starting out at a very young age in this game (not that he was the only one) but never was he tempted to do any drugs. I believe he would have a drink once in a while but other than that this man was all business. We started doing deliveries far and away. At first, I was apprehensive, but the money was good, so we grew in that part.

But one day out of the blue Blanks come to my house looking a little apprehensive and tells me we lost a shipment somewhere in the Midwest. I'm like "we going to war?" These people are not ones to take it lightly if they get shorted in any way, shape, or form. He says "nah, don't trip I got it covered" so I don't worry about it, but it got me to thinking. Not that I wasn't already thinking, shit in my head was swirling like never before. Yes, Gang Law had me caught up in the game for years now and although I was still committed, I was feeling all sorts of confused about what I was thinking. These thoughts were very strong and wouldn't go away.

We traveled all the way to the other side of the world on a secret mission once. Got paid a pile of money for it, but it still didn't feel as exhilarating as it did back in the day, plotting a mission, carrying it out, and completing the mission. Things for me were changing and changing very fast, I wasn't as quick to punch someone in the face like I used to be, but I still did it, and to be honest, I don't believe it was my age either, I was in as good a shape as ever, maybe even better. I just didn't see any fun in it anymore. Here I am a grown ass man. I even got a job to keep the state people off my back.

But still doing dirty work for someone in another country, someone I never met, yet I was risking my life, and freedom among other things. Something about this didn't feel right anymore, I'm not sure if it ever did, I just know that this is what I was into for most of my life. I didn't go into this blindly. I went into this with some way-out thoughts of retiring early and living in the Bahamas. A small place on the beach with a small boat wasn't too much to ask for after all the shit I waded through for most of my life. Listen, we had the game sewed up from both ends, but in the back of my mind things were swirling. Could it be my age making me think differently or what? Not sure but I was thinking oh so differently now.

My boy Blanks was into so many ventures that I couldn't keep up with all of them. I was busy with my own bullshit, but we had made commitments to each other therefore I needed to stay abreast of his daily madness. By now he had relocated to another city but would commute almost on a daily basis. It was business as usual but that's what it seems all it was, we used to laugh at shit all day, even when we needed to crack a head or two

I loved this young man, he was as unique as anyone I've ever met, but something in our souls was changing, I believe he was reaching for a different star and I'm pretty sure that's what amplified our difference of opinion in this crazy ass game we'd been playing for the last decade.

We never crossed one another in the wrong way, sure we had differences, but nothing that we couldn't work out. But as I rode the wave that was cursing through my tired brain, we sorta drifted apart in our ideologies preferences where I wanted to chill and watch a movie, he would rather make money in some fashion or other.

To this day we have a mutual respect for one another. I believe this is why he didn't argue when the time came.

CHAPTER

As I was saying, my mother was starting to get sick and fall down a lot. I ended up getting caught doing some bullshit. I had to crack some fool in the mouth over some stupid shit he pulled when he was tagging along with a good friend of mine to a very important man's home. (Again, without divulging too much) My good friend had gone to visit him and decided to bring along this idiot for some unknown reason. Now this was a man whom I loved and respected very much, and this idiot, whom I didn't even know but was my homeboys' neighbor of sorts, decided to steal a little trinket from this man's home when he thought no one was looking. Turns out the man's granddaughter saw him slip the item into his pocket.

I could never understand why one would steal from someone's home if they are welcomed into it. But unfortunately, being addicted to drugs makes one do stupid stuff they normally wouldn't do in similar circumstances. So, when the issue came down the pike and I was asked to handle it, because conflict of interest according to my friend prevented him from handling it, I was more than happy to accept it. I knew I could have sent any one of my guys, but I thought about it and decided that I would do this myself. As I had mad love and respect for this man, I also totally agreed with my friend on his conflict-of-interest situation.

It was a major mistake on my part, but it is what it is, and I ended up breaking this punk ass mother fucker's face. The cops had been on me for a while now and since this was the only thing, they could make stick; they stuck it to me for a couple of years. I did about 2 on it and came home, but this time things seemed different, I was sure I could step right back into my role as leader of the pack and set up my shops.

But after all that had been running through my head before I went in, these 2 short years gave me an ample amount of time to let my head figure shit out. Don't get me wrong, I was in jail doing time and as such I was a Southsider, so I still had to carry myself as one. I ended up paroling from the hole after some shit jumped off with our Northern Mexican enemies. Seemed one of them didn't like something a Southsider did and next thing you know a fight breaks out in the chow hall and that led to a full-scale riot between the 2 groups and my "influential" ass ended up in the hole 9 days before my release date. So, upon my release, 30 days later, I headed home and said goodbye to the prison life as I knew it.

I was done. I could not go through that bullshit again. I did it 5 times which is to say I fought against the court system five times and lost each time. In this game, usually when one goes away, everything built seems to dissolve and such was the case here I'm only talking about my neighborhood here. My business with blanks was a different department. But upon going to jail, I let it be known that it would be a free for all until I came back to claim what is rightfully mine. All the rules and regulations I had set in place not only for my crew but for the safety of the Barrio children and old folk. Remember my job was to take care of the neighborhood just like all those that came before me, which weren't too many, but each and every one of them had what it took to take charge, and see to it that the neighborhood was safe, and I did it to the best of my ability when it was my turn. When I did come home and made my presence known, most of my workers were ready to go.

But something had changed in me, I seemed to not want this life anymore. Yes of course I was happy to be back but after the bullshit I had seen in there, everything seemed different, something I was subconsciously unaware of but somehow had wanted. My mind set was different this time. The term "this time" has always struck me as an odd one because as a youngster growing up first in the hood then behind the walls, I would hear it a lot. "This time when I get out" or I'm not going back, this time" and to me that was kind of setting you up for failure in some weird way. It seemed like one was prepared to go back, then ready for another chance.

While I was away for this short time, I had seen some fucked up shit in there, not prison violence which was always around, no this was way different. We were sitting at the 'bench' which is where all the southern folk hung out at during yard time even though we had control of the entire yard. We would play cards; pinochle was a favorite of mine.

As we were playing a game one of the fellas was called to the office over the loudspeaker, so he walks over to the office and was gone for about 5 minutes tops, when he walks back up to the bench with this fucked up look on face. I ask, "what's wrong ese, you looking kinda messed up." He answers with a deep hurt in his voice, saying "my mom died". We all gathered around him giving him support in his time. He then says, "I walked in the office and the pinchi huda (fucking cop) just blurts it out "your mom just died" then he adds "like it wasn't shit!"

Now people you all have to understand that to us Chicanos, the feelings we hold for our mothers is sacred, and I'm sure pretty much everyone on the planet feels the same. I personally have gotten into numerous fist fights throughout my life over some idiot saying something about my mother, and to be told "your mother just died" by some fucking guard who has no respect for you, sees you as a fucking number, scum of the earth, is really something that can fuck with your head. That wasn't the worse part.

5 minutes after they break this fucked up news to him in the most fucked up way possible. They then call him back to the office. He walks back and as soon as he walks in, they gaffle him up, which is to say 3 cops grabbed him as soon as he walked into the office and handcuff him and take him to the hole (Administrative Segregation). Now this is some fucked up shit. First, you're told you mother is dead then you get handcuffed and locked in a cage with no access to a phone to at least call your family. This can, and will tear at your very soul, giving you the feeling of being powerless to help loved ones, to be there for them.

Most would argue that "he's in jail" or "he has no rights". That maybe so, but that's not the issue here, the issue is that one's mother has just passed on and as the great king Priam once said, "even enemies can show respect!" For me I just kept thinking about what could be going through his mind at this point, locked in a cage not knowing, not being able to talk with family. Why did they do him like that? Why would they slam him in the hole? He hadn't done anything wrong. Yes, he's in jail, but at least he was behaving, doing his program.

One goes to the hole for breaking the rules or whatever else that is deemed a danger to the security of the prison. But finding out your mother is dead is not, at least I think, a reason to go to the hole. But go to the hole he did and was forced to deal with the loss of his mother alone with the pressure of doing it not knowing anything. It really hit me having witnessed this treatment of a fellow convict. It came to light that the state of California in their infinite wisdom locked him down because they figured he was a Southern Mexican, the most violent prisoner the state has walking their prisons here in beautiful California. Most likely he would go on a rampage and like the saying goes, 'fuck with one bean you going to have to fight the whole burrito' and so to avert any and all problems this one man could potentially cause, this man went to the hole until he calmed down. Now this theory of theirs was never proven therefore I believe it was a chicken shit thing to do after telling him his mother had died.

My own thoughts towards my mother came rushing in and I said to myself "this shit aint happening to me" no fucking way was I going to let this happen to me. Commitments were made by me, to me, not giving thought to my business on the outside. Which brings me back to the swirls in my head. I loved what I was into, I loved my hood, I loved the people living in my neighborhood, but things seemed different now after I got out.

If I went this new way, what would happen? What would be the outcome for my guys? For my neighborhood? The safety I had been providing for the last 30 years. How would my business partners react? These were some troubling thoughts going around in my head. I worried about my mother, every time the ambulance would come for her. I would go into this deep corner of my mind. These thoughts about life that been evading me all my teen and adult years.

I lost my father at a very young age and Tony followed shortly after. Yes, during the Gang Wars I saw plenty of death, but these were guys that just like in the military, signed up for this shit. We knew what we were getting into. Sure, we didn't want to die but it was the luck of the dice each and every time we walked out that front door. I remember once one of my homeboys' moms told me that when her son walked out that front gate he didn't belong to her anymore until he came back. I am in no way belittling my homeboys or my enemies. They all died gruesome deaths. They were all buried with honor & respect. Their memories are remembered by their families. This was just different.

I'm talking about the thoughts I had when my mother would be taken to the hospital. Everything I had been through, the ass kicking's by cops, the time spent in jail, the battle wounds all over my body. All this and more had brought me to this point in my life, to watch my mother deteriorate before my eyes, was something my heart of stone was not ready to deal with, something I don't think I could have dealt with. But somehow, I knew I would have to deal with this in due time and to be honest during all the madness of what was my life, I always thought my mother would bury me. I even think that she thought this too for a while at least. She sure prayed a lot for me, mostly for my soul that is to say if I had one. I'm pretty sure moms was no fool. I'm sure she was aware of the bullshit I was into no matter how hard I tried to be discreet around her. A mother knows is what I've heard, whether it is true or not I'm not sure, but now that I'm older I know a father knows for sure.

My mother had been through so much in her life even in her early life in Mexico, she told me once that it (Mexico) had treated her very badly. She went through her first marriage there, lived with a very wealthy family but was treated very badly by her sisters-in-law. Her first husband was some rich guy who just could not keep it in his pants. He loved my mother very much which was a disappointing issue to his sisters which I guess viewed my mother as just one of his playthings but when he would get out of bed at 2am just to get her a glass of water. They really freaked so it was then that they would treat her very bad whenever he was away. I'm not sure just what they did to her, but you have to imagine a 1940's Mexican country, with 3 or 4 evil sisters plotting against a young country girl.

This continued for their short marriage until one day he just never returned to their hacienda having been killed during one of his adventures out and about in this Wild West country just a few years after their own revolution. And she was left to fend for herself with 2 young boys. Add to that meeting a good-looking young cook in Texas, where she had gone to look for work trying his damndest to sweep her off her feet. She just wasn't into that as she had left 2 young boys back in the old country with her parents while she worked to support them from this side of the border. When she did decide to give this young man a chance, I'm pretty sure they both had no idea that they were about to unleash a nightmare for the small town they chose to live in. But such as it was and my mother withstood all that shit during her time as my mother.

For her to watch all the madness I went through as a young kid to teenager then young adult. To the full-grown terrorist, I had become. Don't misunderstand I was only a terrorist to those that fell on my wrong side. I was a well-mannered man with morals, dignity, and respect for my elders. I saw what I did as a profession. I actually detested violence it just so happens that I was good at it and knew it was a very good tool to have in the line of work I did for a living. She stood by as the parole Gestapo wanna bes' would tear up her house while the cops dragged me away in chains. It was all a surreal feeling whenever this happened, but it was all part of the game.

So, like I said my mother went through a lot in her life and now that she was fading away right before my eyes my mind would take trips and open folders in my head that showed me life in different ways. I could not comprehend it even though whatever it was it was trying very hard to change that which is the inner workings of my mind. My mother aside I would still have to deal with my position in the Barrio, my partnership with Blanks. I knew I was near the end of my career; I knew a change had to take place. But how would I deal with it, I didn't yet know. Until then it would have to be business as usual.

CHAPTER

The real estate, the food business, the cars, the money, the trips, were all fine and dandy. But it was getting to the point where it wasn't fun anymore. What was it about this life that was losing its appeal to me? I had it all, I had a nice shinny car to drive around in, I had plenty of dates with females, money to blow on goodies, nice clothes, and expensive dinners. It seemed like all the stuff I was doing was just going through the motions or something because in reality I would wake up and do my thing conducting business as usual in the neighborhood along with Blanks' business.

But around this point in time as I was saying, my dear mother was becoming very weak and fragile. I would pamper her because I remember once way back in the day my mom had said to me in Spanish, she said "son, behave so that I may die happy" I responded in Spanish also "I don't like that deal moms, if you gonna die, I'm not gonna behave." I was so entrenched into the gang scene, the drug game, taking care of the neighborhood, that everything else was insignificant to me.

I mean the threat of going to jail or the threat of someone shooting me or harming one of my loved ones was something I was willing to accept, to stay the course I was on. Yes of course there would be major repercussions if something like this ever happened. If one of my children were ever hurt because of me or my house was ever shot up!

Shit would hit the fan. I also believe people were well aware of this. But I honestly believe that there was something other than my bodyguards' protecting me and my family. Something more incomprehensible to anyone, because I have to admit, some of the bullshit I done pulled in my day should have gotten me killed a damn long time ago. I went as far as I could go on the dangerous side of this lifestyle.

Don't misunderstand me here I'm not talking spiritual shit here or at least I don't think I am I'm just saying that it couldn't be just luck that kept me alive all this time. Yes, I had skills to do the stuff I was doing; I had trained all my life for this shit. From the beginning with Bugs, then my karate adventure, these things and even the riding around Tony and I did as little kids on our homemade bikes gave me the skills and mentality, I needed to become the man I had become.

I knew at an early age that this was what I wanted to be. Everything I had envisioned as a teenager of what it would be like had come to pass. I had earned all the respect I wanted, I had made peace with my family, and they understood what I was and who I was as it pertained to the Barrio. My children were in my life again and in a very big part of it also.

They seemed well adjusted to being Gangland Royalty. They were well aware that "Father" was a man of respect and in business if only in the hood and not some corporation in downtown. They were well in tune to what life was about on the other side of the tracks as well as in the Barrios. They were under no illusion of whom or what I was. They never saw nothing dirty; maybe a guy gets socked every once in a while. But other than that, I was the man they sat down to dinner with every night, talked about their day at school, and sports with my son; I would even attend their school functions.

I remember when my boy was graduating from the 5th grade, I had bought matching suits for him and me, but the fact remained that the majority of my business was conducted at night I was usually asleep till way past midafternoon. Said graduation day was no exception. Sure, enough come 1pm I was sleeping in my room with 2 guards outside. And for my boy Rob to make it all the way to my bedroom door, that had to be important.

I remember his voice calling my name, and when I woke up, he said something like "isn't Rene' graduating today?" I ask, "what time is it?" he says "1 o'clock" I remember jumping out of bed and washed up. I had no time to put on my suit it would have taken me an hour to get dressed in that monkey suit. So casual gang member attire it is. We bounced to the school where the ceremony was in full swing. We made our way to the standing area by some bushes.

I see my son sitting in the front roll wearing his little Italian cut suit, but the look on his face was not the happiest of faces one would think until his eyes came to rest on me standing there as he was looking around the audience. He broke into the biggest smile of the day, which in the end made everything I did well worth the risks I was taking.

Where was I, oh yeah, let me see if I can figure it out, and explain what it is I'm trying to say here. I don't think it was God who kept me alive all this time. How, can it be? I wondered if I even understood the definition of God. Is he or she a being of good and love and other things that would make a guy like me gag, and if not all, then most of my days had been filled doing bad stuff, so why would this God be protecting me? One would think that for sure he would have let any one of those fools I was banging on kill me. Was it someone from the great beyond looking out for me and keeping me alive all this time? If this was the case, then who was it? Could it be one of my long-gone homeboys from back in the day? Was it my father? Could it have been Tony? Or Bugs? Or maybe it was a combination of these?

I would feel warm and fuzzy if this was the case, but I wonder what about at the beginning of my adventures when all these people were still alive? Who or what was watching out for me then? There were times I would be hiding in the bushes after doing some horrific shit to these enemies of mine, all the while 8 to 10 rival gang members were looking for me to end my life and somehow, I always ended up getting away. Of course, I could run, jump fences, and especially beat a cop on any obstacle course better than most. And that's what I'm getting at, how I can do the stuff I did so recklessly so bold and crazy and still walk away unscathed.

Does it seem strange that I would willingly put myself in these dangerous situations? Yes, I had accepted the consequences way before I went out there. All of us did, first we were neighbors, then elementary school friends, then Jr. High homies, and eventually we became fully fledged gang members although, I still can't for the life of me, remember when we actually became a gang, but because society gave police the power to regulate where regulating was needed and to classify in accordance with their policies, we became documented. I love how then and today they used fancy words to label one.

The fact remained that no matter what the situation was every once in a while, I would be in one where it seemed like there was no way out but yet somehow, I always found a way out. Could it be destiny? Is destiny even true? One does not think about shit like this when it is happening. Oh no we are too busy staying alive. The adrenalin that flows through one as one runs through the night, running through yards, over fences, sometimes hiding under cars. All while being chased by someone that wants to take your freedom or your life, is an exhilarating feeling, kind of strange explaining it here.

Many, many times this would happen to me, and to be honest here, the heights that I was able to jump, or the open spaces I was able to cover before being seen. Seemed to me then and now to be extraordinary. There is no other way to explain this. So, who or what could have been looking out for me, keeping me out of harm's way?

Yes, during these times, I did get hit, and stabbed, and once my leg was grazed by a bullet as I walked home from the city bus stop. But those are stories for another time, right now I'm trying to help you to grasp the myth or reality of how one was able to avoid the really bad things like the loss of body parts, crippled or worse, death. All that happens to one in this crazy game called "La Vida Loka". The battlefield is a battlefield anywhere if one's life can be lost in anger or for whatever reason one finds himself on it. All I know is that my stubbornness kept me going back for more!

Even after all I seen, I still played the game. Never once thinking about how I survived only knowing that I was going back if I made it through this night. But looking back now I do wonder, and think what could it have been? I did grow up Catholic, and then during my wondering years I converted to Christianity. But eventually I saw the hypocritical parts of both these factions and turned away from all religion. And for the most part I never really was too much into religion and this is why when I speak of spiritual shit happening in my life, I'm just speaking in terms that don't have religious implications.

But try as I might I still seem to be implicating religion, and if not religion, then just God into this equation I'm trying to explain here. Could it be just mere luck that kept me alive and got me through these very dangerous situations? Or was there more to it than that? I really believe in my heart of hearts that there was something more than just luck. Was it luck? Was it someone from my past that is now gone? If so, then who was it before them? Was it God? Was I just that good at my craft that I overcame such incredible obstacles? I leave it up to you the reader to decide.

CHAPTER

At the beginning of this story, I said I was the youngest of 7 kids, and to this day I am amazed at this one little fact. I come from a good family. My Father was a hard-working decent man who provided for his family as long as he was alive. I remember the stories he would tell me as a child about growing up in O'l Mexico, he was so proud of the fact of where he came from, and I think he was real happy his sons were able to get down there and see his birthplace. He was a chef by trade; he also dabbled in life insurance, growing up in the neighborhood I was referred to as the insurance man's kid. But through it all he was a true Mexican by blood. Granted he was a poor kid growing up, but he loved Mexico to no end. I never met his father (my grandfather) but what could my grandfather have said to my dad that made him such a proud Mexican. I sometimes wondered.

I'm sure Mexico is in no way the same now as it was way back then. But here in America is where he came to raise a family of his own; even raised 2 boys that weren't his biologically, he loved them, nonetheless. He did an awful lot of drinking towards the end of his life, but his decency never wavered; he loved his wife and children to the very end. I remember the last day I saw him alive. He was sick throwing up blood and was very weak, but he managed to wash up, and dress himself in his cowhide jacket, his cowboy hat, and his boots (I still have them nicely put away to this day.). His heart was a Vaquero since he was a youngster growing up in the deserts of O'l Mexico. With his blessings we watched as he walked up and out to a waiting car to take him to the hospital.

My parents were very young adults when my father died, leaving my mother with five kids at home. We lived in a small Barrio house with small rooms, but we were comfortable and happy. Two of my older brothers had left home years before, both had decent jobs and their own families to worry about, but they were there to help carry my fathers' coffin to his grave. My mother, bless her heart, took on the challenge like nobody's business.

I swear that woman has seen more bullshit than any mother should have to. First, she buried the man she loved while she was still in her mid 40's, and then she saw her youngest son become a living nightmare not only within the family but soon after that I went on a drug induced haze for many years tearing shit up throughout the neighborhood, and she stood by me no matter what.

Along with having her house raided over 10 times in 20 years, and I'm talking bullet proof wearing, Gestapo boots, and guns at the ready raided, it was funny though how they would surround the entire block before moving in and I would still get away from them. I know it pissed them off to no end. Some of the cops would even have bets about if I was going to get arrested that day. This was a vicious game we played. She never complained, at least not to me. But like I said I came from a good family. All my brothers were fairly good guys, I'm sure they had their moments in their day, the only difference between them and I was that they grew up and saw the real world for what it is and went that way.

I just kept going the direction that was laid out for me by my other brothers, Bugs & Tony. My mother also had 2 beautiful daughters, both with hearts of gold. They both married military men, one even had a son go to the military.

So how the hell did I go the way I went? Some would say it was peer pressure, but think about that for a minute, I was a 10-year-old kid. How many of you at the ripe young age of ten were being pressured into stealing car stereos, square lights or fighting to prove your strength on a daily basis? I'm sure I wasn't the only one in this world doing that shit at this age, but this isn't some 3rd world country I'm talking about here. I'm talking about the good o'l U.S. of A., and I'm pretty sure I was the only one in my neighborhood at that age doing this shit.

It seems peer pressure isn't at fault here. No, I pretty much chose this route on my very own. Could there be something mentally wrong with me? I don't think so, at least I hope not. So here I am seeing life from a different perspective not knowing which way is up or which way I should go. Being on the level I was on, playing on the field I was playing on made it rather difficult to comprehend the decision I was facing. For years I worked this criminal ideology like a job in the regular world. I started out a laborer, worked my way up just like anyone else in this game.

And just like any corporation, skills, attitude, and ambition, will get one promoted. Please don't misunderstand me, the criminal ideology I speak of here, is in no way played by the same rules that the real working world plays by. The concept is the same, but the rules are very different. Ambition in the real world will let you betray someone's confidentially and still be friends. In this criminal world ideology, one must stand straight in their ways or there will be consequences to pay.

In the regular world, one can work for years and fuck people over time after time and still be able to show up every day for work. In the world that I have been a part of for so many years now pulling that kind of shit will get one fucked up. Sure, in the working world one could complain to his superiors but big whoop!... what is that gonna do?

I only say these things because I've seen it with my own eyes. I've seen the lies one puts forth to save their own ass over a lower worker. Don't get me wrong this kind of shit goes on in the underworld also only there if you get caught doing that, the shit will definitely hit the fan and not in the liar's favor. Having been part of both worlds opened my eyes to many, many things. I now know that no matter how hard one tries in the underworld, the other side always wins.

Sure, you might get away with shit for a while but one way or the other you will lose. I also know that one can work to the best of his ability in the work world and move up and be a decent person to his fellow workers and family. And of course, there is nothing wrong with that at all. But I have to admit those snakes in the workforce that I spoke of earlier are very good at what they do and have years of practice doing it.

So, in the end after all these thoughts, I'm going to have to choose one world or the other there will be no both sides for me. It would be very, very confusing for one to try and juggle on both sides of the fence between these two worlds.

The differences are too great. The outcomes for similar issues have very different consequences in these worlds. I hope I don't confuse you with the "two worlds" reference. But there really are two worlds we live in. One is the underworld and the other is the normal world. Some people are fortunate enough to never have to deal with the underworld. Some people live in the underworld and never associate with it. I'm happy for those people. But for those of us who do live there and deal with it daily. It can be a real headache. Now to choose one or the other at such a late part of the game is tricky.

CHAPTER

March 24th, 2013, the day that broke my stone heart in ways that I never thought could ever happen. It literally brought me to my knees. My dear sweet mother had passed away and went from this earth to find my dad whom from my understanding never left her side since his death 34 years earlier if that fortune teller was to be believed. To find the words for this next chapter is going to be one of the toughest challenges I've had during my lifetime, and as you might already know I've pretty much traveled the road to hell a couple of times.

Yes, I made it back in one piece, but some damage was done here and there. I've seen death so much that nowadays when I do bring myself to actually attend a viewing or funeral for someone in my life, I just stand out front and talk to people as they arrive, I rarely ever enter the actual funeral home. Death to me is a weird concept, I've studied many different religions throughout my life in the penal system, I've spoken with Muslims, Buddhists, Catholics' & Christians, and they all seem to have the same idea about the afterlife just different ways of getting there.

The last time I saw my mother her eyes were open; she was in the ICU of our local hospital. They had come for her at home on a Saturday morning and she lasted just shy of 24 hours more. I remember Saturday night walking into her room and seeing her just lying there with her eyes open and staring at no one in particular but yet seeing everything. When she saw me, we made eye contact then as I neared her, I said "ya duerrmete ama" I kissed her forehead and walked out. Everything seemed liked a movie, slow motion and what not.

I remembered one of the last times she was in the hospital I saw my first born, whom my mother damn near raised by herself when he was just an adolescent thanks to my ass always being either in jail or out running the streets. I had come walking around one of the hospital hallways and saw him sitting in a chair or bench I don't remember which, but he was sitting there with eyes full of tears.

I said, "what the fuck you crying for?" You have to remember I was strict as hell with my kids and spoke very, very bluntly to them. He answered "man, that's my grandma". But before he could continue, I said, "we the men of this family". I guess that was all I had to say, but I believe I did say more, but this young man took in some air and his chest hardened and he stood up.

I remember telling him, that there was a time and place for us, but right now we had to be strong for all those in the waiting room who came when the call was made that the matriarch of the family was on her way out according to the doctors. He understood and walked with me as we started heading back towards the rest of the family members at the hospital.

Then as we rounded one corner on our way to the waiting room, we saw his sister sitting there crying and I said "what the fuck you crying for? We the men of this family…" and my son says, "dad that shit ain't gonna work on her" so I said, "yeah you right" But as faith would have it even though the doctor had given her less than 20% chance of making it through the night. She awoke the next morning with severe problems, but she didn't die, and it was a long 6-month journey to fully recover from this sickness that almost took her and she was able to come home.

But not this time. When they took her this time it was different, something felt different, the atmosphere was different. I felt very apprehensive about it. The call went out to those who mattered, but I felt something inside me that just didn't feel like the other times.

In the last 20 years of my mother's life, she had been in the hospital at least twice a year for a week here or a week there, but towards the end it would be a month at an old folk's home. She made her rounds there, at different convalescent homes. The first time she was sent to one I had to sit with her for an hour to convince her that we weren't going to leave her there.

Eventually it became just like the hospital stays she was comfortable with knowing it was for her health and not being abandoned by her family. She would take to their exercises and impressed them for a lady of her age. And just for good measure she would always walk out on her 2 feet. So, when they took her that morning my life was about to take a turn that maybe I knew was coming, maybe I didn't but came nonetheless it did.

Everyone that showed up during the day started leaving around midnight. When I left and had gone home after seeing her for the last time even though I didn't know it yet. It was like 10 PM, I remember seeing my son there and saying to him, "remember when I said we can't cry because we are the men of this family? Not this time, if you want to cry, cry". Why would I say that? This time must have felt different, although I wasn't quite sure yet that this was the end for my mother.

Something inside of me felt weird, weak, and like I was headed for some unknown reality. I felt like it wasn't gonna be OK this time. Deep down inside I was hoping it would, but my animal instinct told me different. I remember my sister saying as much. "She's gonna be OK, just like the last time", and I said to her "I don't know sis, she's really sick" but my sister was adamant that she would be OK. We had been through this many times before.

I went home to try and get some rest, but my Barrio business was at hand, so I took care of what needed to be to be taken care of for that night. And eventually came back around 5 in the morning, only an ex-sister-in-law and a niece were there in the waiting room. I told them to go home and get some rest, then it was just me by myself in that big waiting room outside the ICU, I fell into a semi sleep but not really with so many thoughts running through my head that sleep was somehow not an option here. Remembering that this was the same hospital my father had died in 34 years earlier.

Some friends from back in the day died here too, I was even in the room when Tonys' mom had the plug pulled on her. It was a freaking odd event to watch the heart monitor with its little lights flashing letting you know the heart rate. Then to watch it as it slowed down, then just the 'Flat Line' when her heart stopped, surrealistic as fuck it was. Watching Tonys sister get up and touch her mother's head was a little too much for me. And I could only turn my head towards the window.

I remember giving her a fitting send off at her funeral, full color guard from the hood for her, all in honor of her sons who couldn't be there. In the home videos you can see the fucking feds in the procession mixed in with all the low-riders and hearse carrying her body to her final resting place next to her husband and son.

At some point, something stirred me around 8 AM, I snapped to and grabbed my cell phone, I called the ICU, and this really tripped me out. Because the nurse who answered didn't say "hello" or "ICU", no, she answered with "I was just gonna call you" in a soft voice, she said "she just passed". Those words still haunt me today!

My mother died at 7:58 AM. I never imagined my life on this earth without my mother, the woman that was solid as an oak, and the only one who never turned her back on me. No matter what I had done. That loved me to the very end. Stood by my side as the cops tore her house apart, looking for incriminating stuff, which most of the time never materialized.

The lady that gave birth to me so long ago not knowing what I would become, loved her little terror unconditionally. Had just left this world and to me seemed like she tapped me on the shoulder on her way up to heaven. As I walked towards the ICU door the nurse opened it and let me in. I walked through it with so much apprehension like I didn't know what to expect. I thank these nurses for all they did. They go through this bullshit everyday dealing with families from all walks of life.

As she escorted me to the room where my mother had slipped away only minutes earlier, I barely caught a glimpse of her feet when my body gave out. I literally just dropped, but like I said, these nurses deal with this shit on a daily basis. I fell right into a chair. Seems like the nurse behind me was expecting this to happen, and had followed me, with an office chair. After falling, I didn't move nor could I have, from that spot and just sat there texting and calling people with the same words over and over again. "She's gone"

I don't know how long I sat there for; my mind went into shock. Everything I had been feeling and thinking about for the last couple of years had just come back in a flood of emotions, thoughts, questions, among just a few things I was turning over in my head. I was in so much pain I couldn't see straight let alone walk straight.

My mother was gone, the one person that trusted me with everything she was. My life was now completely different with my day starting out this way; with the knowledge that I would never see her or hear her voice again. The way she would roll her eyes when I would say some outlandish thing to her, we had a way-out relationship. My mother always had a soft spot for the outlaw brand of man.

There was another outlaw in the neighborhood that came before me. He was actually my idol growing up. My mother would cover for him as well. She would hide him when the police were looking for him at his parents' house across the street from ours. Although she had stopped cooking years ago, every once in a while, she would cook up some soup or chicken in red sauce. I would never again enjoy watching her pop those little bubbles on the wrapping inside of packages that would come to the house from time to time.

I will forever be thankful for my sister Charay, not actually my blood sister, but my sister, nonetheless. She was the first to arrive at the hospital when I called those that I was able to call. She was there in that time that I was trying to come to grips with what was unfolding before my eyes. If there was anyone, I needed at that time it was her. She had come into our family in the early 90's, how, why, or what the reason was I don't know. And to be honest I don't care, but I can say this, and that's that it was one of the best decisions I ever made in my life.

Whether it was my business side or family side, Charay had my back. I'm afraid that she might even have jumped in front of a gun and take a bullet for me had the situation called for it. A more loyal friend hasn't been found. If anyone knew me better, she was 2nd only to my mother. I remember one of my other sisters would try and get her drunk so she would then be able to question her about our dealings in the Barrio. It never worked but it wasn't from lack of trying by my dear sister Duvina.

The time was here, the day I needed to make my decision was at hand, I know now that the choice I made here would forever alter not only my life but those around me. I had a lot of people depending on me and for many reasons they were there. Some were part of my criminal life, some were my home life, and some were my Barrio life I even now had a work life that was a fucking joke to me because I didn't need the money but yet I was enduring the ignorance of the work world compared to my world.

I would have to rethink my life's motives and how was this gonna affect me personally, if I gave up what I thought would be the normal world and stay the course I have been on for so many years, the course that I trained for, the course that had brought me more ass kicking's by cops that I care to remember. The course that gave me the money and power I had craved since before I had pubic hair.

Or I could give up the life that has given me so much for a world I was barely getting to know. Would I survive in this new world? Don't get me wrong or misunderstand, when I say survive, it is in by no way, shape or form the same as to survive in the world I'd lived in for the past 40 years. Would I be able to hold a job and live the same way I have lived for so long? Would I, or could I, adjust to the rules of this world. A world I was now looking into and really taking serious for the first time. A world I didn't like very much. Add to that, that I had a baby on the way.

My head was spinning like nobody's business. But I welcomed this decision that needed to be made. I think it was one of my biggest challenges. I've made life altering decisions for people in the past. But this would be a first for me. By that I mean I had recruited many, many soldiers in my time in the Barrio and would decide if this individual was actually cut out for this madness. And if they weren't, I would advise them to return to school or look for a job and get away from this world because it was not for them. Most would, and some actually came back to thank me years down the road for changing their lives.

My mother was gone, she died on a Sunday morning, and we buried her a few days later. I never looked at her in that box. It was too damn hard. How could I look at the one person in my life that I could always count on? I remember I did glance at the coffin though, during the wake, and noticed it had pretty roses painted on the corner, a touching touch. My brothers and nephews carried her. I followed behind the casket with a couple of my best and oldest friends.

The whole day was surreal, yes, I was there but I wasn't. I remember my oldest brother saying, "when this is over, I'm going home" and for a long time I didn't know what he meant. At first, I thought he was going home to his place after the funeral. Apparently, everyone was invited to one of my sister's place for food and talk. As I was not in a social mood whatsoever, I headed back to the Barrio to my mother's house and I have to say that my people from the Barrio were there for me, they came and brought carne asada, beer, and soda, as I was never much of a drinker of beer. They comforted me on this very hard and cold day. But it was more than that; I didn't want to be around anybody. But these were not just anybody's they were my people, and sometimes that means more than blood. It's a harsh thing to say but it be like that sometimes, you know.

The death of my mother had brought about change. Change that would have life altering events for not just me but for the many people that were in her life, but this was my life and those around me that I was concerning myself with. I'm sure from the oldest of my brothers to my two sisters. This one death would forever alter their lives just as the death of our father did.

My father's death had come at a time when I was young, much younger than my brothers and sisters and maybe I wasn't as able to deal with or handle it as my siblings had done. Or at least that's the feeling I'm getting now, because if I remember correctly, we or at least I never talked to anyone about my feelings about the death of my father. I turned to the streets and dealt with it that way.

Again, death to me has been a constant in my life among other crazy elements and I have dealt with it as it came and sometimes, I dealt with it differently than the last. But I've dealt with it on my terms. Now here I was confronted with the death of my mother. A man 49 years old, war torn, from running the streets for almost 4 decades with many people following my every move to advance their own, I took everything into consideration and weighed everything in my life.

The biggest weight though I believe was my newborn baby that slid into my life just 3 short months after my dear mother had passed away. It was with a girl I had met year's earlier but had ended on a bad note. But as fate would have it, she fell into my lap one night, one thing led to another, and the good Lord blessed us with a beautiful baby boy. I remember something from my bible reading days, and that was that if God took something from you; He would replace it.

Whether that is true or not I chose to believe that was the case here. My new son has kept me grounded and kept me from going on a rampage. What did I have to lose if I had gone on one anyway? I could've went off and settled old scores and took this shit to another level. Nobody would have given a fuck. They would have just thought it was typical me. But my decision had been made,

I chose to leave the world I had known for so long, the world that I had aspired to be in since I was a 10-year-old boy still watching cartoons and believing in the crying lady. I chose to join the workforce. A world that I despised in many ways, for many reasons but felt the challenge worth taking. I would give it a shot, I would go to bed early, pack a lunch in the morning and go work 8 hours a day and become a contributing "Member of Society". I mean why not? I've done pretty much everything else to this society during my time in the Barrio. To the people of Mi Barrio, it's been an honor serving you, to my business partners, it's been a pleasure. I'm sorry for many things, but I'll never be sorry for believing in the Barrio Life story.

ABOUT THE AUTHOR

Nano is a 58-year-old Mexican/American born in San Diego, California. He attended all his schooling in the San Diego area, graduated from High School in 1984. After doing many prison terms, drugs and everything that comes with Gang Life, Nano retired from that way of living, attended College and earned an Associate Degree in Business Management & Accounting.

Today Nano has over 25 years drug free and lives a quiet life away from the mean streets in the Barrios of Southeast San Diego with his youngest son. After working numerous jobs since his release from prison, Nano has been working for an environmental company in the Hazardous Materials Industry for the last 15 years.

EPILOGUE

In the year 2022, I find myself living a quiet life out in the burbs, away from that crazy life in the Barrio I left behind so many years ago. Many, many years away from the drug dealing days, and even more years far removed from the Gang Life that had surrounded my every waking moment. Do I have regrets? Sure, but I believe the choices one makes are the ones that are for the better of those around them and not just for the individual. In the year that my mother died I was already in the workforce like I said learning the ways of that world.

But it wasn't until after her death that I put all my effort into it, to survive there and regain some normalcy to my family. It was tough at first, but I fell into a pretty good routine, I wake up at 4 and am out the door by 6 every day. As in all adventures it didn't start out easy. No sir I didn't just wake up and say "OK I quit" it's not that simple, and just like my first adventure I would need help. I got help in this one too, starting with the Jewish guy from Chicago, and then there was the man that opened the first door for me. And a slew of other people that helped push, pull, or guided me along the way.

It was a journey that I honestly thought I would never take because the life I had known never even hinted at the idea of it. But in the end, it is the only journey that has given me more riches than money and power could ever give. It gave me Family, and peace of mind. Life for me has been a learning experience almost every day one learns something new.

Back in the day it was try to stay alive, and then after it was protect those that can't. Today is much more, easy going, more smiles. People used to say I never smiled, and well to be honest I didn't have much to smile about and life there in the Barrio wasn't all ice cream and soda, but things have changed since then. I've come into a place in my life where I don't have to always keep looking over my shoulder. I enjoy the peacefulness of living away from the gunfire, the high-speed police chases, and the helicopter flying overhead with its search light on. I remember saying "ah music to my ears" when it would fly over my mom's house in the Barrio.

Those days are long gone, the road of life has taken me far away from the madness, do I miss it? Yes, if I'm to be honest. But the real question here is: "was the choice I made the better of the 2?" I believe it was, I'm no spring chicken anymore. I've lost more friends throughout the years. I've even lost siblings during these changing years. So, to continue down the path I was on for so many years and tempting the hand of fate was illogical,

I'm comfortable in my skin, and I'm comfortable with my life. If I can change, I'm sure there are many out there that can change too. Just follow a simple plan and it will get you there. To be a productive Member of Society, all one has to do is find a job, and don't let pride get in the way. Start at the bottom because that's all there is. I truly believe all one needs is a chance.

Be honest in all you do. Don't try and play both sides of the fence, it won't last. Have patience in all things, it will come. But more importantly, be humble in your life. I'm not saying run out and join a church and yell praises to the Gods, I'm just saying be normal, no more hardcore way of thinking. This world we live in isn't like the old days, just like cowboy gunslingers of the Wild West had their time, guys like us had ours.

In the end all one wants out of life is to be happy and live in peace. It's not going to come looking for you, you will have to earn it. Take what you know about honor, respect & loyalty, and push that into work and your attitude towards this lifetime and maybe you too can become the person you should have been all this time. Remember every day is a blessing.

CONTACT

Nano S,
e-Mail: ReachNanoS@gmail.com